JAVA FROM ZERO TO PROFICIENCY
(BEGINNER)

A step-by-step guide to learn Java.

Patrick Felicia

JAVA FROM ZERO TO PROFICIENCY (BEGINNER)

http://learntocodewithpat/Java

Copyright © 2019 Patrick Felicia (Revised Edition)

All rights reserved. No part of this book may be reproduced, stored in retrieval systems, or transmitted in any form or by any means, without the prior written permission of the publisher (Patrick Felicia), except in the case of brief quotations embedded in critical articles or reviews.

Every effort has been made in the preparation of this book to ensure the accuracy of the information presented. However, the information contained in this book is sold without warranty, either expressed or implied. Neither the author and its dealers and distributors will be held liable for any damages caused or alleged to be caused directly or indirectly by this book.

First published: February 2019

Published by Patrick Felicia

CREDITS

Author: Patrick Felicia.

Patrick Felicia is a lecturer and researcher at Waterford Institute of Technology, where he teaches and supervises undergraduate and postgraduate students. He obtained his MSc in Multimedia Technology in 2003 and PhD in Computer Science in 2009 from University College Cork, Ireland. He has published several books and articles on the use of video games for educational purposes, including the Handbook of Research on Improving Learning and Motivation through Educational Games: Multidisciplinary Approaches (published by IGI), and Digital Games in Schools: a Handbook for Teachers, published by European Schoolnet. Patrick is also the Editor-in-chief of the International Journal of Game-Based Learning (IJGBL), and the Conference Director of the Irish Symposium on Game-Based Learning, a popular conference on games and learning organized throughout Ireland. He has also published books on coding with Java through the creation of games.

Technical Reviewer: Garth Flint

MORE BOOKS BY PAT

JavaScript from Zero to Proficiency (Beginner) [1st Edition]

C# from Zero to Proficiency (Beginner) [1st Edition]

Unity from Zero to Proficiency (Beginner) [3rd Edition]

Support and Resources for this Book

A companion website has been set-up for this book, where you can download the full project for this book, with all the code used throughout the book, so that you can check your own code against the code solutions.

To avail of this content, you can open the following link:

http://learntocodewithpat.com/Java/

This site also provides you with the opportunity to subscribe to a mailing list and receive:

- Your book in the pdf format (FREE copy) so that you can open it on any computer.

- Regular updates and tutorials on Java.

- Coupons to receive more than 30% discounts on some of my books.

This book is dedicated to Mathis & Helena

PREFACE

This book is part of a series entitled **Java from Zero to Proficiency**. In this book series, you have the opportunity to learn Java programming from scratch and to become proficient in this popular programming language.

In this book entitled "**Java from Zero to Proficiency (Beginner)**" you will discover how to quickly get started with Java; you will learn about how to use variables, methods, conditional statements and you will also write your own code.

WHAT YOU NEED TO USE THIS BOOK

To complete the project presented in this book, you only need to install Java Software Development Kit (SDK) and an Integrated Development Environment of your choice.

In terms of computer skills, all the knowledge introduced in this book will assume no prior programming experience from the on your part. Although this book includes programming, you will be guided step-by-step. So for now, you only need to be able to perform common computer tasks such as typing, and opening and saving files.

WHO THIS BOOK IS FOR

If you can answer **yes** to all these questions, then this book is for you:

- Are you a total beginner in Java programming?
- Would you like to get started fast with Java concepts?
- Although you may have had some prior exposure to Java, would you like to delve more into Java?

If you can answer yes to all these questions, then this book is **not** for you:

- Can you already easily code in Java?
- Are you looking for a reference book on Java?
- Are you an experienced (or at least advanced) Java programmer?

If you can answer yes to these three questions, you may instead look for other books in this series. To see the content and topics covered by these books, you can check the official website: **http://learntocodewithpat/Java**.

IMPROVING THE BOOK

Although great care was taken in checking the content of this book, I am human, and some errors could remain. As a result, it would be great if you could let me know of any issue or error you may have come across in this book, so that it can be solved and the book updated accordingly. To report an error, you can email me (**learntocodewithpat@gmail.com**) with the following information:

- Name of the book.

- The page where the error was detected.

- Describe the error and also what you think the correction should be.

Once your email has been received, the error will be checked, and, in the case of a valid error, it will be corrected and the book page will be updated to reflect the changes accordingly.

SUPPORTING THE AUTHOR

A lot of work has gone into this book and it is the fruit of long hours of preparation, brainstorming, and finally writing. As a result, I would ask that you do not distribute any illegal copies of this book.

If some of your friends are interested in the book, you can refer them to the book's official website (**http://learntocodewithpat.com/Java**) where they can either buy the book, enter a monthly draw to be in for a chance of receiving a free copy of the book, or to be notified of future promotional offers.

TABLE OF CONTENTS

1 Introduction to Java programming 20
    What is Java 21
    Choosing a code editor 22
    Installing Java 23
    Installing BlueJ 25
    Creating your first application 27
    Introduction to Java syntax 36
    Statements 37
    Comments 40
    Variables 43
    Using variables 46
    Operators 47
    Conditional statements 49
    Methods 53
    Scope of variables 57
    A few things to remember when you create your applications (checklist) 61
    Best practices 63
    Level roundup 64

2 Customized Data types & Structures 69
    Working with String variables 70
    Working with number variables 75
    Switch statements 77

Table of Contents

    Single-dimensional arrays 81

    Single-dimensional arrays 89

    Loops 91

    Constants 96

    Level roundup 100

3 Object-Oriented Programming & Classes 104

    Classes 107

    Defining a class 108

    Accessing class members and variables 110

    Constructors 120

    Static members of a class 125

    Inheritance 129

    Accessing methods and access modifiers 139

    Polymorphism (general concepts) 140

    Packages and Namespaces 143

    Lists 144

    HashMaps 148

    Level roundup 151

4 Creating a Word Guessing Game 154

    Detecting and processing the user input 155

    Choosing random words 163

    Tracking the score and the number of attempts 165

    Level Roundup 171

5 Thank you 175

CONTENT COVERED BY THIS BOOK

- Chapter 1, *Introduction to Java programming*, provides an introduction to general programming concepts. including Java syntax, variables and methods. In this chapter, you will start to create your first application and combine variables, and methods.

- Chapter 2, *Customized Data types & Structures*, delves deeper into Java and explains how to employ customized methods, structures and data types to optimize your code. You will use loops and arrays to create a quiz, and learn how to work with Strings and numbers with built-in methods.

- Chapter 3, *Object-Oriented Programming & Classes*, explains key Object-Oriented concepts such as classes, polymorphism, inheritance, or encapsulation. This chapter will show you how to create your own classes and apply some common Object-Oriented concepts.

- Chapter 4, *Creating a Word Guessing Game*, combines all the skills that you have learned to create a word game.

- Chapter 5 summarizes the topics covered in this book and provides you with more information on the next steps to follow.

How you will Learn from this Book

Because all students learn differently and have different expectations of a course, this book is designed to ensure that all readers find a learning mode that suits them. Therefore, it includes the following:

- A list of the learning objectives at the start of each chapter so that you have a snapshot of the skills that you will gain.

- Each section includes an overview of the activities covered.

- All the activities are step-by-step, and you are also given the opportunity to engage in deeper learning and problem-solving skills through the challenges offered at the end of each chapter.

- Each chapter ends-up with a quiz and challenges through which you can put your skills (and knowledge acquired) to the test. Challenges consist in coding, debugging, or creating new features based on the knowledge that you have acquired in the chapter.

- The book focuses on the core skills that you need. While some sections go into more detail, once concepts have been explained, links are provided to additional resources, where necessary.

- The code is introduced progressively and it is also explained in detail.

FORMAT OF EACH CHAPTER AND WRITING CONVENTIONS

Throughout this book, and to make reading and learning easier, text formatting and icons will be used to highlight parts of the information provided and to make the book easy to read.

SPECIAL NOTES

Each chapter includes a resource section, so that you can further your understanding and mastery of Java; these include:

- A quiz for each chapter: these quizzes usually include 10 questions that test your knowledge of the topics covered throughout the chapter. The solutions are provided on just after the quiz.

- A checklist: it consists of between 5 and 10 key concepts and skills that you need to be comfortable with before progressing to the next chapter.

- Challenges: each chapter includes a challenge section where you are asked to combine your skills to solve a specific problem.

Author's notes appear as illustrated below:

> Author's suggestions appear in this box.

Code appears as illustrated below:

```
public int score;
public String playersName = "Sam";
```

Checklists that include the important points covered in the chapter appear as illustrated below:

- Item1 for check list.
- Item2 for check list.
- Item3 for check list.

How Can You Learn Best from this Book?

- Talk to your friends about what you are doing.

  We often think that we understand a topic until we have to explain it to friends and answer their questions. By explaining your different projects, what you just learned will become clearer to you.

- Do the exercises.

  All chapters include exercises that will help you to learn by doing. In other words, by completing these exercises, you will be able to better understand the topics and gain practical skills (i.e., rather than just reading).

- Don't be afraid of making mistakes.

  I usually tell my students that making mistakes is part of the learning process; the more mistakes you make and the more opportunities you have for learning. At the start, you may find the errors challenging, or you may find that your application does not work as expected until you understand what went wrong.

- Challenge yourself.

  All chapters include a challenge section where you can decide to take on a particular challenge to improve your programming or skills. These challenges are there for you to think creatively and to apply the knowledge that you have acquired in each chapter using a problem-based approach.

- Learn in chunks.

  It may be challenging to go through five or six chapters straight, as it may lower your motivation. Instead, give yourself enough time to learn, go at your own pace, and learn in small units (e.g., between 15 and 20 minutes per day). This will do at least two things for you: it will give your brain the time to "digest" the information that you have just learned, so that you can start fresh the following day. It will also make sure that you don't "burn-out" and that you keep your motivation levels high.

FEEDBACK

While I have done everything possible to produce a book of high quality and value, I always appreciate feedback from readers so that the book can be improved accordingly. If you would like to give feedback on this book, you can email me at **learntocodewithpat@gmail.com**.

1
INTRODUCTION TO JAVA PROGRAMMING

"Everybody in this country should learn to program a computer, because it teaches you how to think"

- Steve Jobs

In this section, we will go through an introduction to Java programming and look at key aspects of this programming language, including:

- It's syntax.
- Variable types and scope.
- Methods.

So, after completing this chapter, you will be able to:

- Understand key concepts related to Java programming.
- Understand how to use variables and methods.
- Create and use your own methods.

> The code solutions for this chapter are included in the **resource pack** that you can download by following the instructions included in the section entitled "**Support and Resources for this Book**".

WHAT IS JAVA

Java is a high level object-oriented language developed by Sun. It is a multiplatform language which means that once it has been written and compiled, a Java application can run on most platforms.

The fact that it is an object-oriented programming language means that a Java programme consists of a collection of objects that interact with each other.

Java is used for many purposes, including the creation desktop or mobile applications or even games.

CHOOSING A CODE EDITOR

In the next sections, you will start to write your own Java code. For this purpose, you will need to use a code editor, and more specifically, an Integrated Development Environment (IDE). These IDEs include all the necessary tools to compile and execute your code, in addition to other options that will speed-up your development and also help you to keep it free from bugs.

Using an IDE will provide you with an easier way to create, organize and check your code, with some of the following features:

- **Text highlighting**: so that you code is clearer to read and to modify.

- **Auto-completion**: so that you don't have to remember the name of all the variables in your code, or the name of some common methods.

- **Error highlighting**: so that some obvious errors are highlighted before you even test your code.

There are many free IDEs available with their advantages and drawbacks, including:

- BlueJ.
- Eclipse.
- IntelliJ IDEA.
- NetBeans.

All these IDEs considered, we will be using **BlueJ** for this book, although you could use any of the other IDEs if you wish. BlueJ is an IDE specially developed for beginners. It won't overwhelm you with too many features, but instead, help you to get started with Java and provide some very useful features along the way that will make your coding clearer, such as class diagrams, or code split into color-coded blocks.

You can download **BlueJ** from the following site: **https://www.bluej.org/**

INSTALLING JAVA

Before you start working with Java, you will need to install the most recent version of the Java Development Kit (JDK). The JDK includes all the libraries that you need to be able to write, compile and run code in Java.

To do so, please do the following:

- Open the following page:

https://www.oracle.com/technetwork/Java/Javase/downloads/index.html

- Look for the latest version of Java SE Development Kit.

- Download the most recent Java SE DK: as this book is being written, the latest version of Java is **Java SE 11.0.2**.

Figure 1-1: Downloading the SDK(Part 1)

- Once you click on the Download button, a new set of options will appear from which you can chose the version that you would like to download, after accepting the license agreement..

[23]

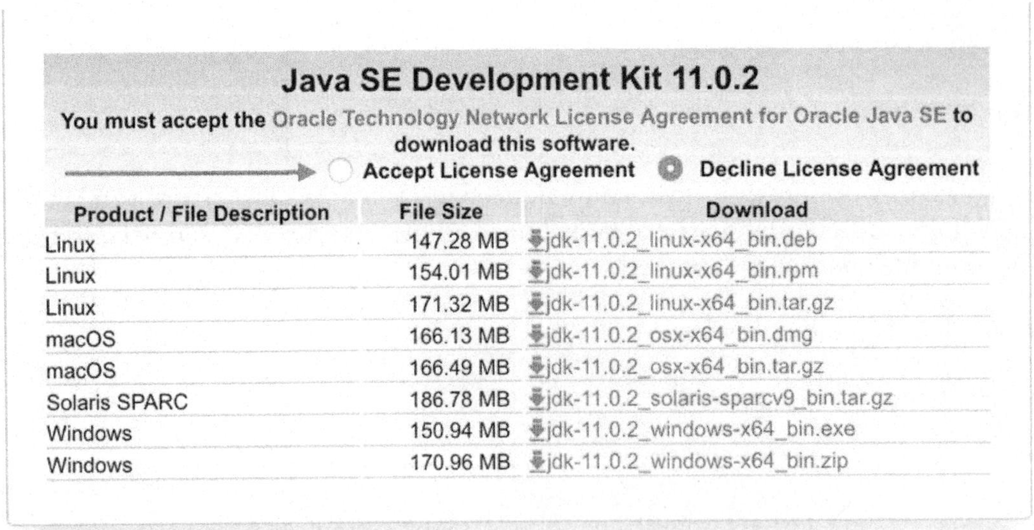

Introduction to Java programming

Product / File Description	File Size	Download
Linux	147.28 MB	jdk-11.0.2_linux-x64_bin.deb
Linux	154.01 MB	jdk-11.0.2_linux-x64_bin.rpm
Linux	171.32 MB	jdk-11.0.2_linux-x64_bin.tar.gz
macOS	166.13 MB	jdk-11.0.2_osx-x64_bin.dmg
macOS	166.49 MB	jdk-11.0.2_osx-x64_bin.tar.gz
Solaris SPARC	186.78 MB	jdk-11.0.2_solaris-sparcv9_bin.tar.gz
Windows	150.94 MB	jdk-11.0.2_windows-x64_bin.exe
Windows	170.96 MB	jdk-11.0.2_windows-x64_bin.zip

Figure 1-2: Downloading the SDK(Part 2)

- Once you have downloaded the software please launch it and follow the instructions.

INSTALLING BLUEJ

Once the Java SDK has been installed, it is time to install **BlueJ**, which is an IDE that you will use to write your code in this book. BlueJ was designed with Java beginners in mind and includes many features that make it easy to create Java applications. So let's install this software:

- Please open the following link: **https://www.bluej.org/**.

- Download the **BlueJ** version that corresponds to your operating system (i.e., for Mac OS, Windows, or Linux).

Download and Install

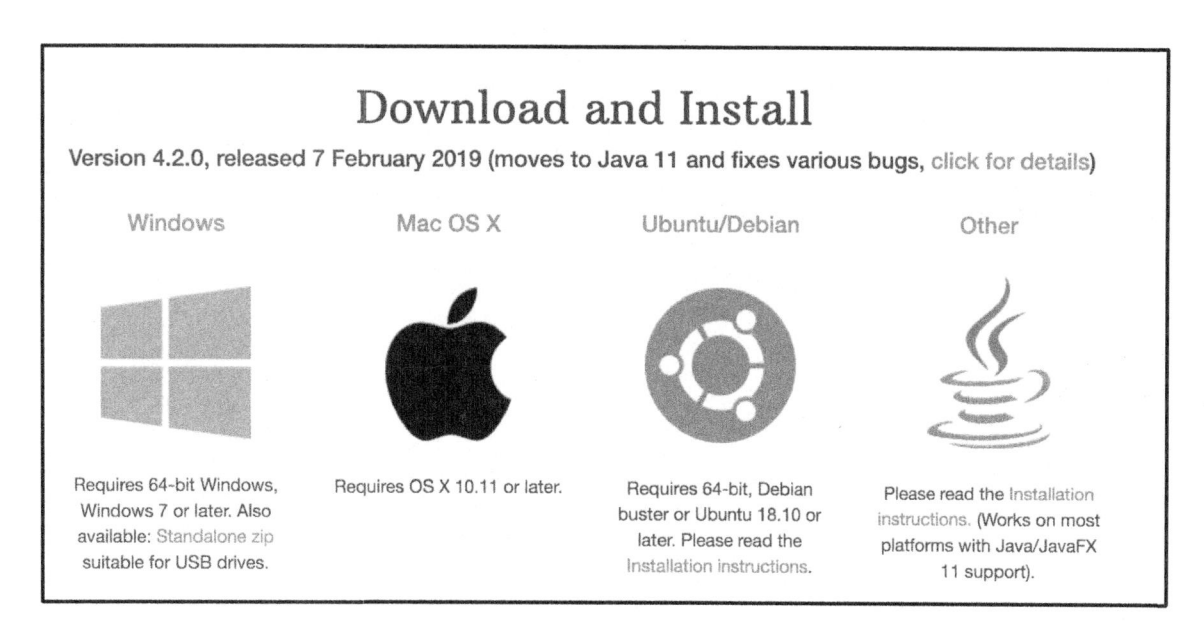

Version 4.2.0, released 7 February 2019 (moves to Java 11 and fixes various bugs, click for details)

Windows	Mac OS X	Ubuntu/Debian	Other
Requires 64-bit Windows, Windows 7 or later. Also available: Standalone zip suitable for USB drives.	Requires OS X 10.11 or later.	Requires 64-bit, Debian buster or Ubuntu 18.10 or later. Please read the Installation instructions.	Please read the Installation instructions. (Works on most platforms with Java/JavaFX 11 support).

Figure 1-3: Installing BlueJ

If you are using a Windows computer:

- Double-click the install file that you have downloaded.

- This will run a standard installation. Follow the instructions on screen. The installer will install the executable bluej.exe.

- If when executing BlueJ you see a dialog box asking you whether you want to block or unblock BlueJ, you may choose not to block BlueJ so that it can be launched seamlessly.

Introduction to Java programming

- The first time you launch BlueJ, and if you have more than one Java version installed on your computer, you will be asked to select your preferred version.

If you are using a Mac:

- Download the installer for Mac (this is a zip file).
- Decompress the zip file; this will create a folder called BlueJ.
- Move the resulting folder to your Applications folder for example.
- You can then click on the icon called BlueJ, to launch this application.

Figure 1-4: Installing BlueJ on a Mac

CREATING YOUR FIRST APPLICATION

After this brief introduction, it is now your turn to code.

So that you get to experiment with your Java code, please do the following after installing BlueJ:

- Please launch BlueJ.

- Once BlueJ has been launched, select: **Project | New Project** from the top menu to create a new project.

- In the new window, please select a name and a location for your project and click "**OK**".

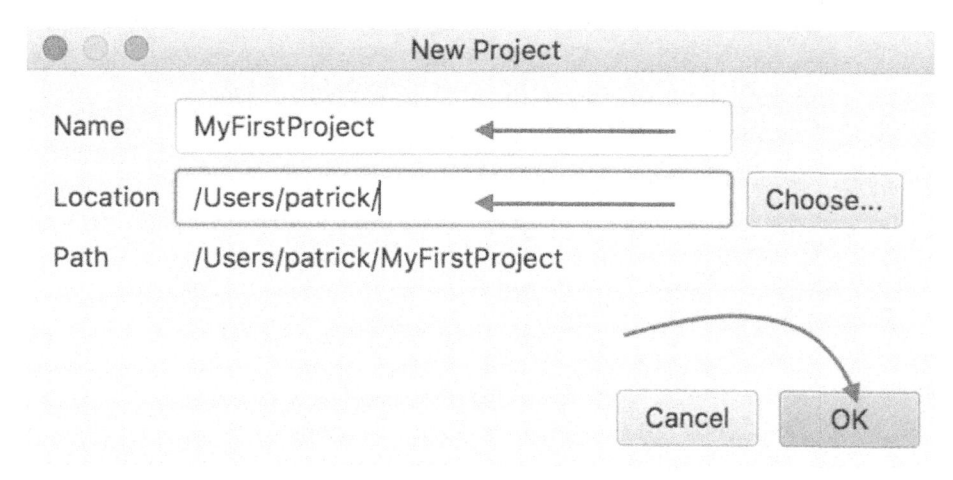

Figure 1-5: Selecting a location for the project

- Once this is done, a new window will appear that will make it possible for you to create your first programme.

[27]

Introduction to Java programming

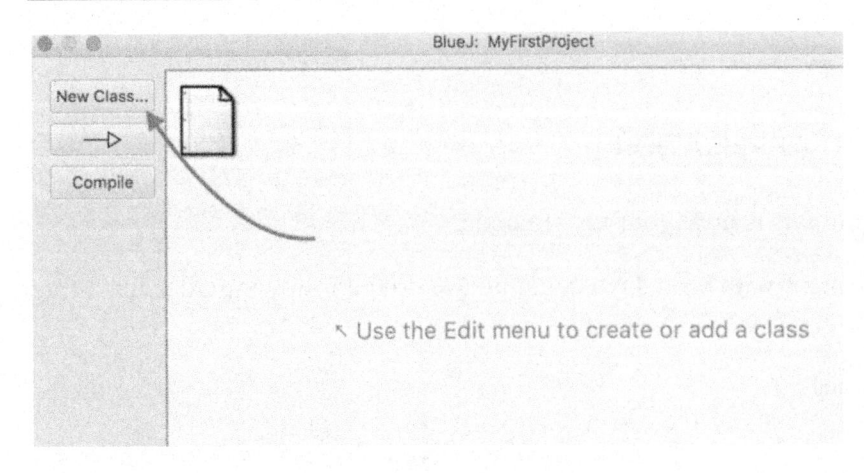

Figure 1-6: Creating your first programme in Java (part 1)

- Click on the button called "**New Class**" that is located on the left-hand side of the window, as per the previous figure. This will open a new window.

- Enter a name of your choice in the text field for the attribute "**Class Name**", leave all the other options as default, and press "**OK**".

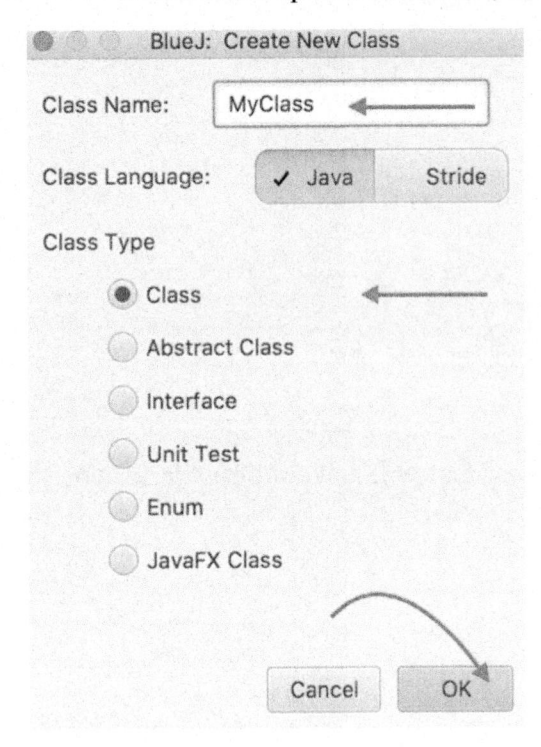

Figure 1-7: Creating your first programme in Java (part 2)

- You should see that a new class called **MyClass** has been created within your project.

[28]

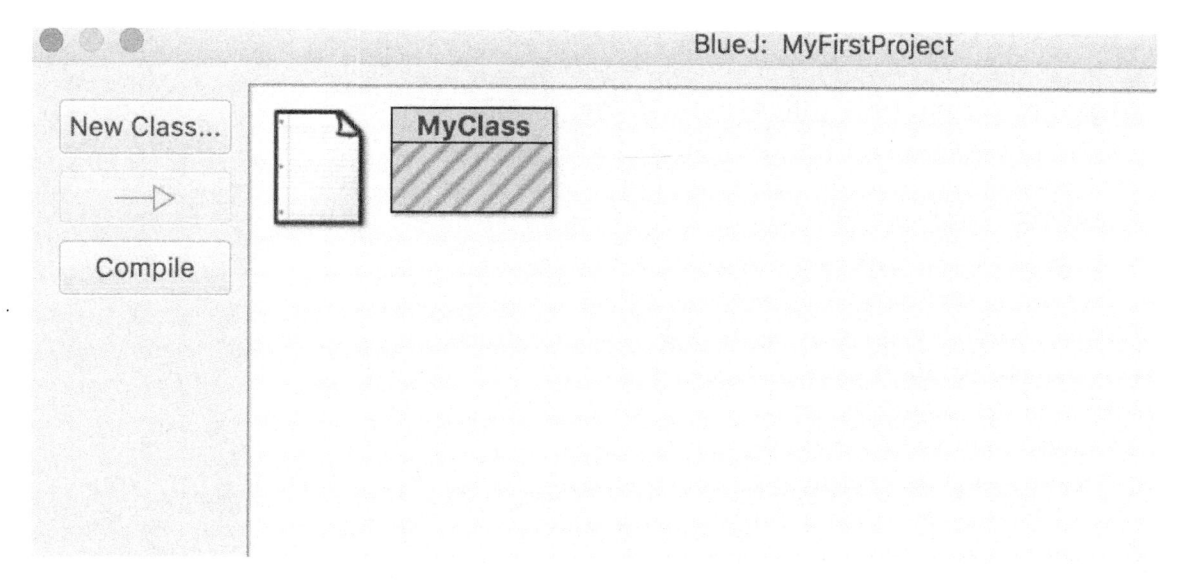

Figure 1-8: Creating your first programme in Java (part 3)

- You can now double-click on the icon labelled "**MyClass**", as per the previous figure.

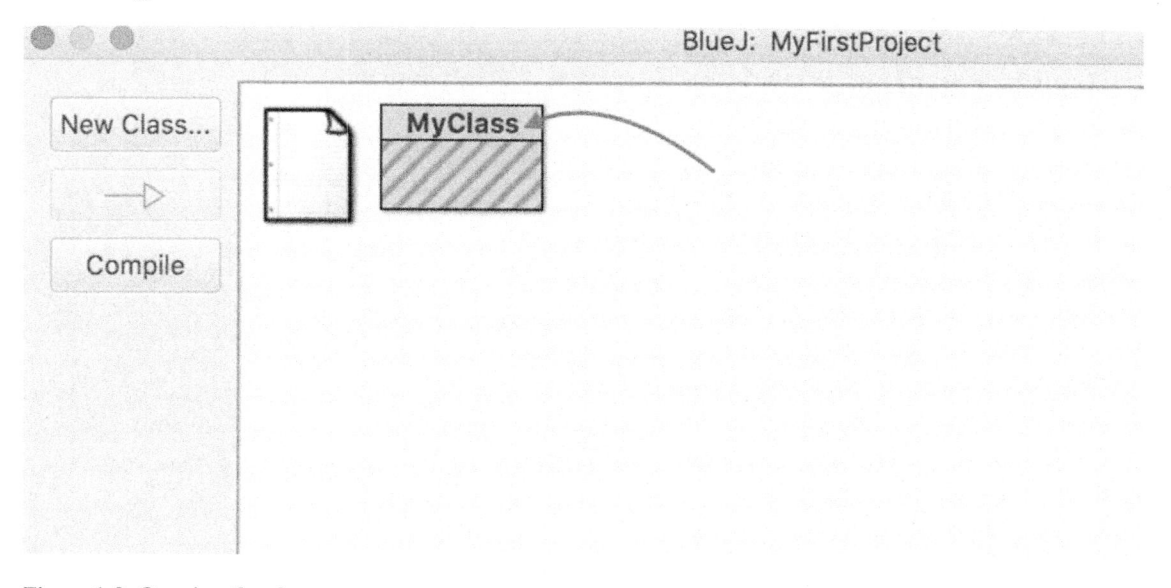

Figure 1-9: Opening the class

- This will open a new window that displays the code that has been created by default for your new class, as follows.

[29]

Introduction to Java programming

```
/**
 * Write a description of class MyClass here.
 *
 * @author (your name)
 * @version (a version number or a date)
 */
public class MyClass
{
    // instance variables - replace the example below with your own
    private int x;

    /**
     * Constructor for objects of class MyClass
     */
    public MyClass()
    {
        // initialise instance variables
        x = 0;
    }

    /**
     * An example of a method - replace this comment with your own
     *
     * @param  y   a sample parameter for a method
     * @return     the sum of x and y
     */
    public int sampleMethod(int y)
    {
        // put your code here
```

```
        return x + y;
    }
}
```

Since we will not be using all this code, please do the following:

- Select all the code (**CTRL + A**).
- Press delete to delete all the code.
- Type the following code instead:

```
public class MyClass
{
  public static void main (String [] parameters)
  {
      System.out.println("Hello World");
  }
}
```

In the previous code:

- We declare a class called **MyClass**. As we will see later, your application will be made of a collection of classes. One of these classes will be the class **MyClass** which the starting point for your application.

- We also declare a method called **main**. This method will be the starting point for our application.

- In this method, and this is the most important part for now, we write the text **"Hello World"** in the console window. This window will be displayed as you execute your code.

You can now do the following:

- Compile and execute this code by pressing the button labelled **"Compile"** from the top of the window.

Introduction to Java programming

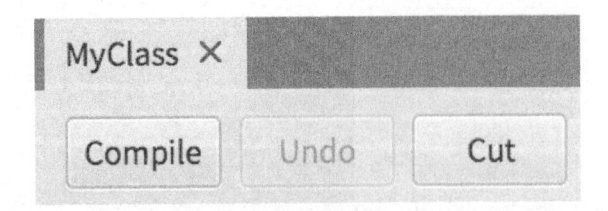

Figure 1-10: Compiling your code

- Check that your code has been compiled properly by ensuring that the message **"Class Compiled – no syntax errors"** is displayed at the bottom of the window.

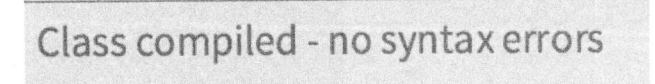

Figure 1-11: Checking for errors

- Run your programme: switch to the **"Project"** window, right-click on the icon labelled **"MyClass"**, and select the option **void main(String [] parameters)** from the contextual menu, as illustrated in the next figure.

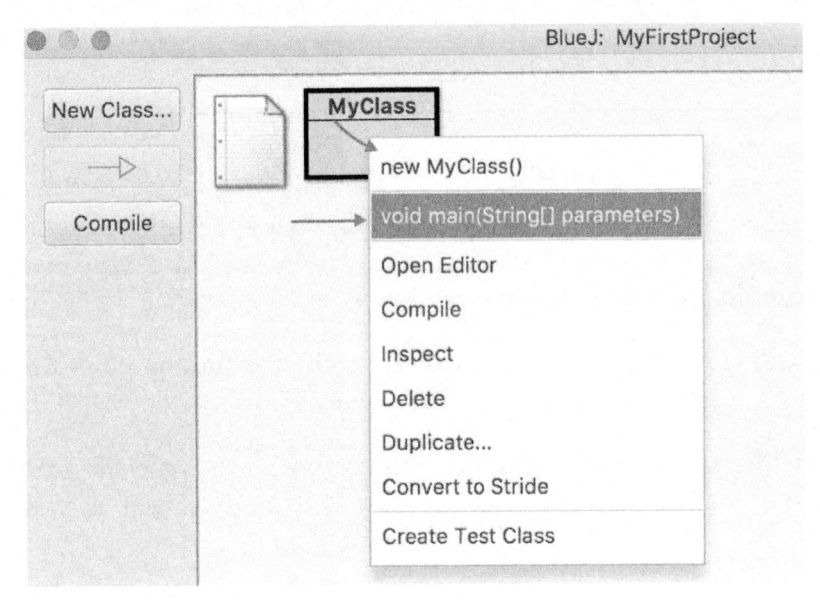

Figure 1-12: Running your first lines of code (part 1)

- A new window will appear asking you whether you want to enter parameters: just press **"OK"** for now.

[32]

void main(String[] parameters)

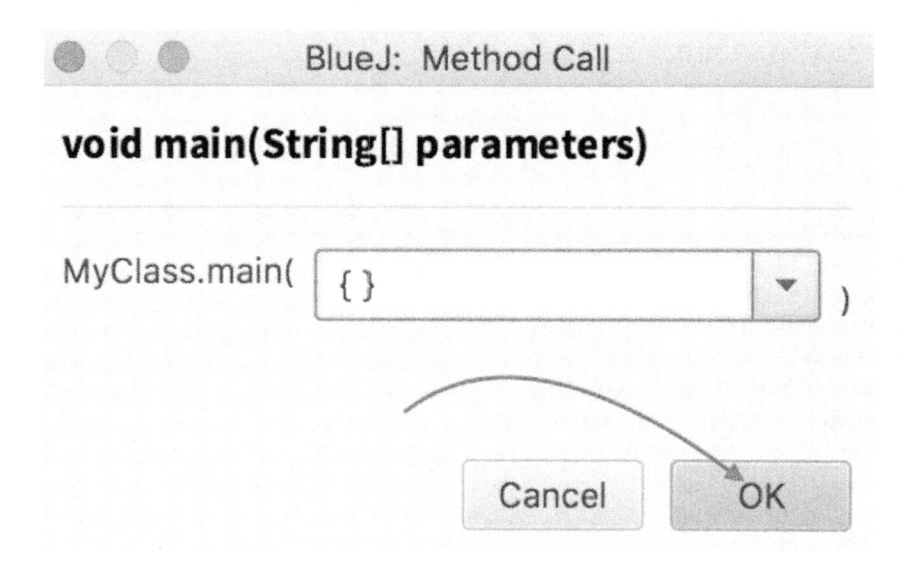

MyClass.main({ })

Figure 1-13: Running your first lines of code (part 2)

- Once this is done, the terminal window should appear as follows.

```
Hello Worlrd
```

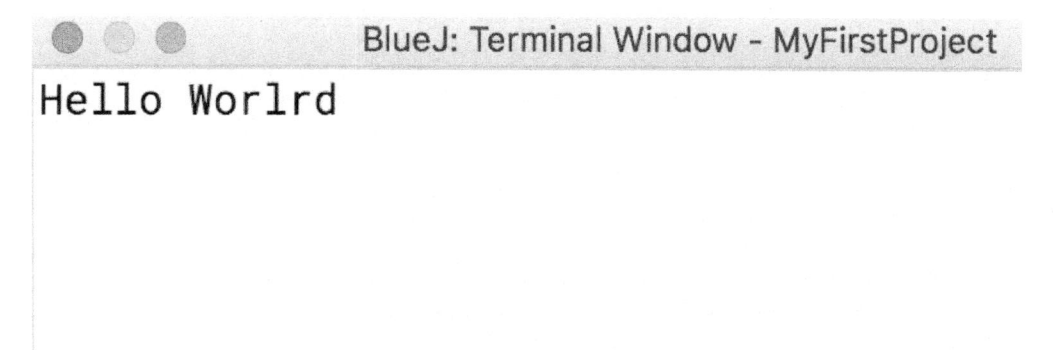

Figure 1-14: Your first console application

As illustrated in the previous figure, the text **"Hello World"** was written and displayed in the terminal window, based on your code.

We could now change our code to display a different message:

- Please close the console window.

- Edit your code and modify it as follows (new code in bold). To edit your code, you can double click on the icon called **MyClass** in the main window.

Introduction to Java programming

```
public static void main(String[] args)
{
    System.out.println("Hello, this is my first line of code");
}
```

In the previous code, we just modified the message displayed in the console window to add the text "this is my first line of code".

- You can then compile and run your code and see the new message: **"Hello, this is my first line of code**" in the console window.

ABOUT COMPILING AND JAVA BYTECODE

When you write your Java source code, it is usually saved as **.Java** file. Once your file is compiled, it is converted (i.e., compiled) into bytecode as a **.class** file. This code, in turn, is interpreted by the Java Virtual Machine (JVM) that is installed on your computer and directly executed or translated into a code that the computer can understand (i.e., machine code) and execute. So, the JVM acts as a translator between your bytecode and the computer. The advantage of this approach is that given that a Java Virtual Machine can be installed on most computers, your code after being compiled into bytecode, can be executed on any computer where the Java Virtual Machine has been installed. You can therefore compile your code once and run the code virtually anywhere.

You may wonder how the JVM is installed. Well, when you installed the Java SDK at the very start of this book, it installed, amongst other things, a JVA Runtime Environment (JRE) that includes the Java Virtual Machine, as well as the Java compiler.

You can see both the **.Java** and **.class** that have been created and compiled in your project, if you navigate to the folder that you have chosen for your project initially. For example, in the next figure, you can see that several files, including **MyClass.Java** and **MyClass.class**, that belong to the current project.

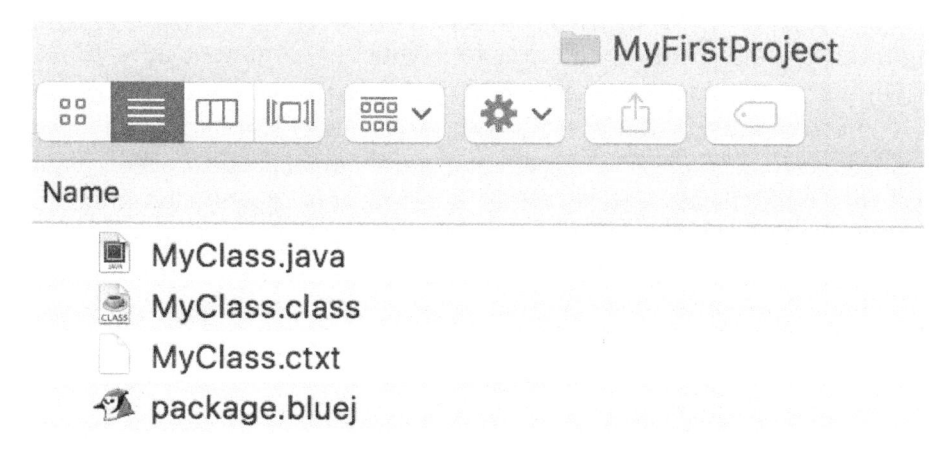

Figure 1-15: Locating the .class and .Java files

INTRODUCTION TO JAVA SYNTAX

Now that you have created, compile and executed your first line of code, let's look at Java syntax.

When you are using Java, you are communicating with the system asking it to perform actions. To communicate with the system, you are using a language or a set of words bound by a syntax that the computer and you know and understand. This language consists of keywords, key phrases, and a syntax that ensures that the instructions are written and (more importantly) understood properly.

In computer science, this language needs to be exact, precise, unambiguous, and with a correct syntax. In other words, it needs to be **exact**.

When writing Java code, you will be following a syntax; this syntax will consist of a set of rules that will make it possible for you to communicate your instructions unambiguously. In addition to its syntax, Java also uses classes, and your Java applications will, by default, be saved as classes.

In the next section, we will learn how to use this syntax. If you have already coded in JavaScript, some of the information provided in the rest of this chapter may look familiar, and this prior exposure to other programming languages will definitely help you.

When programming in Java, you will be using a specific syntax to communicate with the system; this syntax will be made of sentences that will be used to convey information on what you would like the computer to do; these sentences or statements will include a combination of keywords, variables, methods, or events; and the next section will explain how you can confidently build these sentences together and consequently program in Java.

STATEMENTS

When you code in Java, you need to tell the system to execute your instructions (e.g., print information) using statements. A statement is literally an order or something that you ask the system to do. For example, in the next line of code, the statement will tell the system to print a message in the **Console** window:

```
System.out.println("Hello Word");
```

When writing statements, you will need to follow several rules, such as:

- **The order of the statements**: each statement is executed in the same order as it appears in the application. For example, in the next example, the code will print **hello**, and then **world;** this is because the associated statements are in that specific sequence.

```
System.out.println("hello");
System.out.println("world");
```

- **Statements are separated by semi-colons** (i.e., semi-colon at the end of each statement).

> Note that several statements can be added on the same line, as long as they are separated by a semi-colon.

For example, the next line of code has a correct syntax, as all of its statements are separated by a semi-colon.

```
System.out.println("hello"); System.out.println("world");
```

- **Multiple spaces are ignored for statements**; however, it is good practice to add spaces around the operators +, -, /, or % for clarity. For example, in the next code snippet, we say that **a** is equal to **b**. You may notice that spaces have been included both before and after the operator =.

```
a = b;
```

- **Statements to be executed together (e.g., based on the same condition) can be grouped using code blocks**. In Java, code blocks are symbolized by curly brackets (e.g., { or }). So, in other words, if you needed to group several statements, you would include all of them within the same set of curly brackets, as follows:

Introduction to Java programming

```
{
    System.out.println("hello stranger!");
    System.out.println("today, we will learn about programming");
}
```

As we have seen earlier, a statement usually employs or starts with a **keyword** (i.e., a word that the computer knows and understands). All these keywords have a specific purpose, and common ones are as follows:

- Printing a message in the **console** window: the keyword is **System.out.println**.

- Declaring a variable: the keyword, in this case, depends on the type of the variable that is declared (e.g., **int** for integers, **String** for text, or **bool** for Boolean variables), and we will see more about these in the next sections.

- Declaring a method: the keyword to be used depends on the type of the data returned by the method. For example, in Java, the name of a method is preceded by the keyword **int** when the method returns an **integer**; it is preceded by the keyword **String** when the method returns a **String**, or by the keyword **void** when the method does not return any information.

- Marking a block of instructions to be executed based on a condition: the keywords are **if** and **else**.

- Exiting a method: the keyword is **return**.

Now that you know more about statements, let's modify your initial code to include more statements:

- Please open the file **MyClass** that we have used earlier.

- Add the following code to it (new code in bold):

```
System.out.println("Hello, this is my fist line of code");
{
    System.out.println("this is my first application");
    System.out.println("This statement and the previous one belong to the same block of instructions");
}
```

In the previous code:

- We have created a block of instructions that starts with an opening curly bracket and that ends with a closing curly bracket.

- Within this block, we have created two statements that display a message in the console window; both statements are ending with a semi-colon.

You can now save your code and run the application; you should see two additional messages displayed in the console window (i.e., the ones that you have just added).

For now, using blocks of instructions may look like it will not make much of a difference to your coding. This being said, blocks of instructions are very helpful, as we will see later, especially when we need to tell the browser to execute a list of instructions based on a condition, for example. This is because, in this case, instead of telling the system to execute each instruction individually, we can instead, ask for a block of instructions to be executed.

COMMENTS

In Java, you can use comments to explain your code and to make it more readable by others. This becomes important as the size of your code increases; and it is also important if you work in a team, so that other team members can understand your code and make amendments in the right places, if and when it is needed.

Code that is commented is usually not executed. There are two ways to comment your code in Java using either **single-** or **multi-line** comments.

In single-line comments, a **double forward slash** is added at the start of a line or after a statement, so that this line (or part thereof) is commented, as illustrated in the next code snippet.

```
//the next line prints Hello in the console window
System.out.println("Hello");
//the next line declares the variable name
String name;
name = "Hello";//sets the value of the variable name
```

In multi-line comments, any code between the characters forward slash and star " /*" and the characters star and forward slash "*/" will be commented, and this code will not be executed. This is also referred as **comment blocks**.

```
/* the next lines after the comments will print the message
"hello" in the console window
we then declare the variable name and assign a value
*/
System.out.println("Hello");
String name;
name = "Hello";//sets the value of the variable name
//System.out.println("Hello World")
/*
    String name;
    name = "My Name";
*/
```

In addition to providing explanations about your code, you can also use comments to prevent part of your code from being executed. This is very useful when you would like to debug your code and find where the error or bug might be, using a very simple method. By commenting sections of your code, and by using a process of elimination, you can usually find the issue quickly. For example, you can comment all the code and run the application; then comment half the code, and run the application. If it works without no errors, it means that the error is within the code that has been commented, and if it does not work, it means that the error is in the code that has not been commented. In the first case (when the code works), we could then just comment half of the portion of the code that has already been commented. So, by successively commenting more specific areas of our code, we can get to discover what part of the code includes the bug. This process is often called **dichotomy**, as we successively divide a code section into two.

Let's use comments in our application:

- Please open the file **MyClass**.
- Modify the code as follows (new code in bold).

Introduction to Java programming

```
public static void Main(String[] args)
{
    //System.out.println("Hello, this is my fist line of code");
    System.out.println("Hello, this is my second line of code");
    {
        System.out.println("this is my first application");
```

In the previous code, we comment the message **"Hello this is my first line of code"** and replace it with the message **"Hello this is my second line of code"**.

Now that you have made these changes, please save your code and run the application; you should see that, this time, the message **Hello this is my first line of code** has been replaced with **"Hello this is my second line of code"**.

We could also use multi-line comments as follows (new code in bold).

```
System.out.println("Hello, this is my second line of code");
{
    /*System.out.println("this is my first application");
    System.out.println("This statement and the previous one belong to the same block of instructions");*/
}
```

In the previous code, we used a multi-line comment. This means that the two lines comprised between /* and */, while they belong to the file, will not be executed.

If you save your code and run the application, you should see that the only message displayed onscreen is **"Hello this is my second line of code"**.

VARIABLES

Now that you know a bit more about statements and comments, we will start to learn more about variables, which are quite important in Java, as you will probably use them in most of your programs to perform calculations or to work with text.

So what is a variable?

A variable can be compared to a container that includes a value that may change over time. When using variables, we usually need to: (1) declare the variable by specifying its type, (2) assign a value to this variable, and (3) possibly combine this variable with other variables using operators, as illustrated in the next code snippet.

```
int myAge;//we declare the variable myAge
myAge = 20;// we set the value of the variable myAge to 20
myAge = myAge + 1; //we add 1 to the variable myAge
```

In the previous example, we have declared a variable called **myAge** and its type is **int** (as in **integer**). We save the value **20** in this variable, and we then add **1** to it.

> Note that in Java the variable is declared using its type followed by its name. As we will see later, we will also need to use what is called an **access modifier** in order to specify how and from where this variable can be accessed.

> Also note that in the previous code, we have assigned the value **myAge + 1** to the variable **myAge**; the = operator is an assignment operator; in other words, it is there to assign a value to a variable and is not to be understood in a strict algebraic sense (i.e., that the values or variables on both sides of the = sign are equal).

To make Java coding easier and leaner, you can declare several variables of the same type in one statement. For example, in the next code snippet, we declare three variables **v1**, **v2**, and **v3** in one statement. This is because they are of the same type (i.e., they are **integers**).

```
int v1,v2,v3;
int v4=4, v5=5, v6=6;
```

In the previous code, the first line declares the variables **v1**, **v2**, and **v3**. All three variables are **integers**. In the second line of code, not only do we declare three variables simultaneously, but we also initialize them by setting a value for each of these variables.

Introduction to Java programming

When using variables, there are a few things that we need to determine including their name, their type and their scope:

- **Name of a variable:** a variable is usually given a unique name so that it can be identified easily and uniquely. The name of a variable is usually referred to as an **identifier**. When defining an identifier, it can contain letters, digits, a minus, an underscore or a dollar sign, and it usually begins with a letter. Identifiers cannot be keywords (for example the keyword **if** cannot be used as an identifier).

- **Type of variable:** variables can hold several types of data, including numbers (e.g., integers, doubles or floats), text (e.g., Strings or characters), Boolean values (e.g., true or false), arrays, or objects (we will see the concept of arrays later in this chapter).

```
String myName = "Patrick";//the text is declared using double quotes

int currentYear = 2017;//the year needs no decimals and is declared as an integer

float width = 100.45f;//the width is declared as a float (i.e., with decimals)
```

- **Variable declaration:** variables need to be declared so that the system knows what you are referring to if you use this variable in your code. The first step in using a variable is to declare or define this variable. At the declaration stage, the variable does not have to be assigned a value, as this can be done later. In the next example, we declare a variable called **myName** and then assign the value **"My Name"** to it.

```
String myName;
myName = "My Name"
```

- **Scope of a variable:** a variable can be accessed in specific contexts that depend on where in the application the variable was initially declared. We will look at this concept later.

- **Accessibility level:** as we will see later, a Java program consists of classes; for each of these classes, the methods and variables within can be accessed depending on their **accessibility** levels, and we will look at this principle later.

Common variable types include:

- **String**: same as text.

- **Int**: integer (1, 2, 3, etc.).

[44]

- **Boolean**: true or false.

- **Float**: with a fractional value (e.g., 1.2f, 3.4f, etc.).

- **Arrays**: a group of variables of the same type. If this is unclear, not to worry, this concept will be explained further in this chapter.

Introduction to Java programming

USING VARIABLES

In this section, we will start to use variables and combine them using statements and operators. So let's get started:

- Please add the following code just after the code that you have previously created, as follows (new code in bold).

```
//System.out.println("Hello, this is my second line of code");
{
    /*System.out.println("this is my first application");
    System.out.println("This statement and the previous one belong to the same block of instructions");*/
}
int dateOfBirth = 1990;
int currentYear = 2017;
int age = currentYear - dateOfBirth;
System.out.println("My age is " + age);
```

In the previous code:

- We have commented the previous code that displayed **"Hello, this is my second line of code"** using the two forward slashes; so this code will not be executed.

- We declare two variables **dateOfBirth** and **currentYear**.

- We then declare a variable called **age**.

- We perform a subtraction between the variable **currentYear** and the variable **dateOfBirth**, and we then save the result in the variable called **age**.

- Finally, we print the text **"My age is "**, followed by the value of the variable called **age**.

> Note that adding a number and a String is equivalent to concatenating these two, so the result of this addition will be a String.

You can now save your code, compile it, and run your application; you should see the message **"My age is 27"** in the **Console** window.

OPERATORS

Once we have declared and assigned a value to a variable, we can use operators to modify or combine variables. There are different types of operators available in Java, including arithmetic operators, assignment operators, comparison operators and logical operators.

So let's look at each of these.

- **Arithmetic operators** are used to perform arithmetic operations including additions, subtractions, multiplications, or divisions. Common arithmetic operators include +, -, *, /, or % (modulo) and their use is illustrated in the next code snippet.

```
int number1 = 1;// the variable number1 is declared
int number2 = 1;// the variable number2 is declared
int sum = number1 + number2;// we add two numbers and store them in sum
int sub = number1 - number2;// we subtract two numbers and store them in sub
```

- **Assignment operators** can be used to assign a value to a variable and include =, +=, -=, *=, /= or %= and their use is illustrated in the next code snippet.

```
int number1 = 1;
int number2 = 1;
number1+=1; //same as number1 = number1 + 1;
number1-=1; //same as number1 = number1 - 1;
number1*=1; //same as number1 = number1 * 1;
number1/=1; //same as number1 = number1 / 1;
number1%=1; //same as number1 = number1 % 1;
```

Introduction to Java programming

> Note that the + operator, when used with Strings, will concatenate them (i.e., add them one after the other to create a new String). When used with a number and a String, the same will apply and the result is a String (for example **"Hello"+1** will result in **"Hello1"**).

- **Comparison operators** are often used for conditions to compare two values. Comparison operators include **==, !=, >, <, >= and >=,** and their use is illustrated in the next code snippet.

```
if (number1 == number2); //if number1 equals number2

if (number1 != number2); //if number1 and number2 have different values

if (number1 > number2); //if number1 is greater than number2

if (number1 >= number2); //if number1 is greater than or equal to number2

if (number1 < number2); //if number1 is less than number2

if (number1 <= number2); //if number1 is less than or equal to number2
```

CONDITIONAL STATEMENTS

While we have looked at simple variables such as numbers or text, and how to modify them with operators, we will now look at conditional statements.

Conditional statements are statements that are performed based on a condition, hence their name. Their syntax is usually as follows:

```
if (condition) statement;
```

This means **if the condition is verified (or true) then (and only then) the statement is executed**. When we assess a condition, we test whether a declaration (or statement) is true.

For example, by typing **if (a == b)**, we mean **"if it is true that a equals b"**. Similarly, if we type **if (a>=b)** we mean **"if it is true that a equals or is greater than b"**

As we will see later, we can also combine conditions. For example, we can decide to perform a statement if two (or more) conditions are true. For example, by typing **if (a == b && c == 2)** we mean **"if a equals b and c equals 2"**. In this case using the operator **&&** means **AND**, and that both conditions will need to be true. We could compare this to making a decision on whether we will go sailing tomorrow.

For example, we could translate the sentence **"if the weather is sunny and the wind speed is less than 5km/h then I will go sailing"** as follows.

```
if (weatherIsSunny == true && windSpeed < 5) IGoSailing = true;
```

When creating conditions, as for most natural languages, we can use the operator **OR** noted **||**. Taking the previous example, we could translate the following sentence **"if the weather is too hot or the wind is faster than 5km/h then I will not go sailing "** as follows.

```
if (weatherIsTooHot == true || windSpeed > 5) IGoSailing = false;
```

Another example could be as follows.

```
if (myName == "Patrick") System.out.println("Hello Patrick");
else System.out.println ("Hello Stranger");
```

In the previous code, we display the text **"Hello Patrick"** if the variable **myName** equals to **"Patrick"**; otherwise, we display the message **"Hello Stranger"**.

Introduction to Java programming

> When we assess true and false conditions, we are effectively applying what is called **Boolean logic**. Boolean logic deals with Boolean numbers that have two values 1 and 0 (or true and false). By evaluating conditions, we are effectively processing Boolean numbers and applying Boolean logic. While you don't need to know about Boolean logic in depth, some operators for Boolean logic are important, including the **!** operator. It means **NOT** or **"the opposite of"**. This means that if a variable is true, its opposite will be false, and vice versa. For example, if we consider the variable **weatherIsGood = true**, the value of **!weatherIsGood** will be **false** (its opposite). So the condition **if (weatherIdGood == false)** could also be written **if (!weatherIsGood)** which would literally translate as "if the weather is **NOT** good".

Let's experiment with conditional statements:

- Please open the file **MyClass**.

- Add the following line at the start of the class

```
import Java.util.Scanner;
```

In the previous code we import the class called **Scanner** so that we can use it in our own programme; this class, provided by Java, makes it possible to read the users' input.

- Please add the following code (new code in bold) at the end of the **main** method:

```
System.out.println("My age is " + age);
System.out.println("Please enter your name: ");
Scanner sc= new Scanner (System.in);
String nameOfUser = sc.nextLine();
System.out.println("Hello "+nameOfUser);
```

In the previous code:

- We write a message that asks the user to enter his/her name.

- We declare the variable **sc**; this variable will be used to capture the information entered by the user. The variable **sc** is of type **Scanner**.

> As we will see later, when we build a new Scanner variable, we need to tell the system where the information it has to process is coming from; in our case, this information is coming from the standard input (i.e., the keyboard) which we refer as **System.in**, hence the following syntax *sc = new Scanner (System.in)*.

- We then declare the variable **nameOfUser**. This variable will then contain the answer (a String) entered by the user.

- We store the name using the method **nextLine**, which is a method provided by Java to read text entered by the user (after the user has pressed the key **Enter**).

- Once the name has been entered by the user, it is stored in the variable **nameOfUser**.

- We then display a message that includes the word "**Hello**" followed by the name that the user has entered.

You can now save your code and run the application:

- Enter a name of your choice using the text field located at the bottom of the window.

- Press Enter.

- A new message should be displayed in the console window with the word **Hello** followed by the name that you have entered.

```
BlueJ: Terminal Window - MyFirstProject
Hello, this is my fist line of code
My age is 27
Please enter your name:
Patrick
Hello Patrick
```

Figure 1-16: Testing your code

- You can then close the **console** window.

Now that we have managed to capture the entry from the user, we will experiment with using conditional statements. So, please amend the code in the file **MyClass** as follows (new code in bold).

[51]

Introduction to Java programming

```
/*System.out.println("Please enter your name: ");
Scanner sc= new Scanner (System.in);
String nameOfUser = sc.nextLine();
System.out.println("Hello "+nameOfUser);*/


System.out.println("What is 1 + 1");
Scanner sc= new Scanner (System.in);
int answer= sc.nextInt();
if (answer == 2) System.out.println("Well Done!");
else System.out.println("Sorry Incorrect Answer!");
```

In the previous code:

- We comment the previous code.

- We display text that invites the user to write the solution to the question **"What is 1 + 1"**.

- We declare a variable called **result**.

- We then ask the user to enter his/her guess. This time we use the method **sc.nextInt()** because the answer will be stored as an integer.

- Once the answer has been entered, it is stored in the variable **result**.

- We then perform a conditional statement based on the value of the variable **result**. If the text entered is **"2"**, then the message **"Well done"** is displayed, otherwise, the message **"Sorry Wrong Answer"** is displayed instead.

You can now save your code, compile it, and run your application, and you should see, as for the previous example, a text asking you to enter your answer to the question "What is 2 + 2".

- After entering the number **2** and pressing **Enter**, a message saying **"Well done"** should appear.

METHODS

Now that you can declare and combine numbers and Strings, it is a good time to start looking into methods.

Methods can be compared to a friend or a colleague to whom you gently ask to perform a task, based on specific instructions, and to return information afterwards, if need be.

For example, you could ask your friend the following: "**Can you please tell me when I will be celebrating my 20th birthday given that I was born in 2000**". So you give your friend (who is good at Math :-)) the information (i.e., the date of birth) and s/he will calculate the year of your 20th birthday and give this information back to you. So in other words, your friend will be given an input (i.e., the date of birth) and s/he will return an output (i.e., the year of your 20th birthday). Methods work exactly this way: they are given information (and sometimes not), perform an action, and then sometimes, if needed, return information.

In programming terms, a method is a block of instructions that performs a set of actions. It is executed when invoked (or put more simply **called**) from the application, or when an event occurs (e.g., when the player has clicked on a button). As with variables, methods are declared and can also be called.

Methods are very useful because once the code for a method has been created, it can be called several times without the need to rewrite the same code all over again. Also, because methods can take parameters, a method can process these parameters and produce or return information accordingly; in other words, they can perform different actions and produce different outputs based on the input. As a result, methods can do one or all of the following:

- Perform an action.
- Return a result.
- Take parameters and process them.

A method is usually declared using two keywords followed by its name as follows:

```
accessType typeOfDataReturned nameOfTheFunction
(listOfParameters)
{
      Perform actions here
}
```

In the previous snippet:

Introduction to Java programming

- The access type defines the scope of the method or, put simply, from where this method will be available (or can be called).

- The type of the data returned can be: void (no data is returned) or any type of data that this method could return such as **int**, **Boolean**, or **String**.

- The previous information is then followed by the name of the method.

- The list of parameters can be empty if this method does not take any parameter. Otherwise, it includes a list of parameters preceded by their type and separated by a comma; we will cover this aspect later.

Using this template, we could, for example, define the following method:

```
public void myMethod ()
{
    System.out.println("hello");
}
```

In the previous code:

- The method is declared as public.
- Its return type is **void**, which means that it does not return any data.
- It takes no parameters.
- When called this method will write the message **"hello"** to the **console**.

A method can be called using the () operator, as illustrated in the next code snippet:

```
nameOfTheFunction1();
nameOfTheFunction2(value);
int test = nameOfFunction3(value);
```

In the previous code, a method is called with no parameter (first line), or with a parameter (second line). On the third line, a variable called **test** will be set with the value returned by the method **nameOfFunction3** which takes one parameter.

Let's create our very own method:

- Please open the file **MyClass**, and comment your previous code as in the next code snippet; to speed up things, and if you are working with Visual Studio, you can select these lines and then press simultaneously **CTRL + /** (or **APPLE + /**).

```
//System.out.println("What is 1 + 1");
//String resultAsString = Console.ReadLine();
//int result = Int32.Parse(resultAsString);
//if (result == 2) System.out.println("Well done");
//else System.out.println("Sorry, wrong answer");
```

- Then add the following code to the **main** method:

```
int myAge = calculateAge(1990);
    System.out.println("My Age is " + myAge);
}
```

In the previous code:

- We declare a variable called **myAge**.

- We call the method **calculateAge**, passing the number **1990** as a parameter.

- The information (or value) returned by the method is stored in the variable **myAge** and then displayed in the console window.

We can now create the method called **calculateAge** by adding the following code after the method **main**.

```
public static int calculateAge(int yearOfBirth)
{
    return (2018 - yearOfBirth);


}
```

In the previous code:

- The method **calculateAge** is declared; it takes one parameter called **yearOfBirth**. So any parameter passed to this method will be referred as **yearOfBirth** within this method.

- This method returns the result of the subtraction **2018 – yearOfBirth**.

- When the method is called, **yearOfBirth** is equal to **1990**; so it will return **28** (i.e., **2018-1990**).

Introduction to Java programming

> Note that the new method called **calculateAge** is declared as static; this is because, the method main is static by default, and that as a result, it can only call a method that is also static. If you forget to declare this method as static and try to call it from the **main** method, the system will generate an error message.

> The main method is static because it is the entry point of the programme, and it is the first method to be called (or invoked) when the application is started. It is **public** because it needs to be accessible from outside the application. Its return type is **void** because it usually doesn't return any data. It includes parameters but these are not compulsory.

Please save your code, and run the application, and you should see the message "**Hello, My Age is 28**" in the console window.

SCOPE OF VARIABLES

Whenever you create variables in Java, you will need to be aware of their scope so that you use it where its scope makes it possible for you to do so. This is particularly important if you use methods, as some variables will be used just locally, whereas others will be used throughout the class or the application.

The scope of a variable refers to where you can use this variable in an application. In Java, in addition to access modifiers that will be covered later in this book, variables can be **member variables** or **local variables**.

- Member variables can be used in a specific class or throughout your application, depending on their access type.

> Put simply, your application will be made of several parts called classes. In our case, the entry point for our application is a class called **MyClass**.

- Member variables can be declared at the start of the class, using the usual declaration syntax, preceded by what is called an access type (we will come back to this concept later on). They can then be used anywhere in the class (and sometimes outside the class also), as illustrated in the next code snippet.

```
class MyClass
{
    public int myVar;
    public void method1()
    {
        myVar = 0;
    }
    public void method2()
    {
        myVar = myVar + 1;
    }
```

In the previous code, the member variable **myVar** is declared at the start of the class **MyClass**; it is then initialized in **method1**, and updated in **method2**. Note that the variable was declared as public, which means that not only is it accessible throughout the class called **MyClass**, but it is also accessible from outside this class.

Introduction to Java programming

- Local variables are declared (and should only be used) within a specific method; hence the term local, because they can only be used locally, as illustrated in the next code snippet.

```java
public void method1()
{
    int myVar;
    myVar = 0;
}
public void method2()
{
    int myVar2;
    myVar2 = 2;
}
```

In the previous code, **myVar** is a local variable to the method **method1**, and can only be used within this method; **myVar2** is a local variable to the method **method2**, and can only be used within this method.

> Note that it is always good to avoid what is called variable masking/shadowing, which occurs when you give a local variable the same name as a member variable in the same file, as this could lead to confusion.

> Classes and member variables can be compared to a city with different clubs and societies. The city is made of these different clubs. Each club has members. Some of these members can only be accessed if you are already part of this specific club where they belong to; other members will be available more publically for people who are not part of the same club. Because some of these members (for example a treasurer) are very powerful and could change significantly the future and safety of the club, you may prefer that not everyone outside the club has access to them, as it would mean that anyone can ask them to make drastic changes to the club. However, all the club members, because they are trusted, could be granted access to this treasurer. On the other hand, each club could have a PR person in charge of promoting the club. In this case, this member could be made public so that anyone outside this club can access them to get information about the club (e.g., opening hours, features, etc.).

So let's experiment with variables and their scope:

- Please open the file **MyClass**.

- Comment the code already present in the **main** method.
- Add the following code to the file **MyClass** (new code in bold).

```
public class MyClass
{
    public static int myMemberVariable;

    public static void myMethod()
    {
        myMemberVariable = 3;
        System.out.println("The value of myMemberVariable is " + myMemberVariable);
    }
    public static void Main(String[] args)
    {
        myMemberVariable = 1;
        System.out.println("The value of myMemberVariable before calling the method is " + myMemberVariable);
        myMethod();
    }
}
```

Introduction to Java programming

In the previous code:

- We declare a member variable called **myMemberVariable**; because it is declared outside any method, this variable will be a member variable and accessible throughout our class.

- It is declared as static because it will be called from the **main** method which is already static by default; and as we already know, a static method should only call a method that is also static.

- We then call the method **myMethod**.

- In the method called **myMethod**, we set and display the value of the variable **myMemberVariable**.

- Finally, when the application is launched, the **main** method is called (as it is the point of entry of our application),

- We set the value of the variable **myMemberVariable** to **1**, and then call the method **myMethod**.

Please save your code and run your application. You should see a message saying

```
The value of myMemberVariable before calling the method is 1
The value of myMemberVariable is 3
```

A FEW THINGS TO REMEMBER WHEN YOU CREATE YOUR APPLICATIONS (CHECKLIST)

When you start coding, you will, as for any new activity, make small mistakes, learn what they are, improve your coding, and ultimately get better at writing your applications. As I have seen in the past with students learning programming, there are some common errors that are usually made; these don't make you a bad programmer; on the contrary, it is part of the learning process because *we all learn by trial and error, and making mistakes is part of the learning process*.

So, as you create your first application, set any fear aside, try to experiment, be curious, and get to learn the language. It is like learning a new foreign language: when someone from a foreign country understands your first sentences, you feel so empowered! So, it will be the same with Java, and to ease the learning process, I have included a few tips and things to keep in mind when writing your applications, so that you progress even faster. You don't need to know all of these by now (I will refer to these later on, in the next chapter), but it is so that you are aware of it and also use this list if any error occurs. So, watch out for these: :-)

- Each opening bracket has a corresponding closing bracket.

- All variables are written consistently (e.g., spelling and case). The name of each variable is case-sensitive; this means that if you declare a variable **myvariable** but then refer to it as **myVariable** later on in the code, this may trigger an error, as the variable **myVariable** and **myvariable**, because they have a different case (upper-case **V**), are seen as two different variables.

- As much as possible, declare a variable prior to using it (e.g., **int myVar**).

- For each variable name, all words (except for the first word) have a capitalized initial. This is not a strict requirement, however, it will make your code more readable.

- For each method, all words (except for the first word) have a capitalized initial. This is not a strict requirement; however, it will make your code more readable.

- All statements are ended with a semi-colon.

- For **if** statements the condition is within round brackets.

- For **if** statements the condition uses the syntax "==" rather than "=".

- When calling a method, the exact name of this method (i.e., case-sensitive) is used.

- When referring to a variable, it is done with regards to the scope of the variable (e.g., call local variables locally).

- Local variables are declared and can be used within the same method.

- Member variables are declared outside methods and can be used anywhere within a class.

BEST PRACTICES

As you will start your journey through Java coding, you may sometimes find it difficult to interpret the errors produced by the browser. However, after some practice, you will manage to recognize them, to understand (and also avoid) them, and to fix them accordingly. The next list identifies the errors that my students often come across when they start coding in Java.

Variable naming

- Use meaningful names that you can understand, especially after leaving your code for two weeks.

```
String myName = "Patrick";//GOOD
String b = "Patrick";//NOT SO GOOD
```

- Capitalize the initial of all words in the name, except for the first word.

```
bool testIfTheNameIsCorrect = true;// GOOD
bool testifthenameiscorrect = true; // NOT SO GOOD
```

Methods

- Use unique (i.e., different) names (for member and local variables).
- Check that all opening brackets have a corresponding closing bracket.
- Indent your code.
- Comment your code as much as possible to explain how it works.

LEVEL ROUNDUP

SUMMARY

In this chapter, we have managed to create your very first applications. You have become more comfortable with the creation of variables and methods, as well as the display of information through the console window. Finally, you also learned how to employ conditional statements so that processing can be performed based on specific conditions. Building on this knowledge, you created simple programs where the user enters information and where the program computes and outputs a result accordingly. So we have covered some significant ground here from no knowledge of Java to creating your first application: well done!

Quiz

It is now time to test your knowledge. Please specify whether the following statements are TRUE or FALSE. The answers are available on the next page.

1. The main point of entry in a Java program is the method calledm**Main**.

2. The **main** method is usually **public** so that it can be called from outside your application.

3. The main method is usually declared as **static**.

4. The command **System.out.println** displays information in the *Console* window.

5. The **Scanner** class makes it possible to read information entered by the user through the keyboard.

6. In Java text values are surrounded by double quotes.

7. In Java a local variable can only be used in the method where it was initially defined.

8. In Java a member variable can be used throughout the class where it was declared.

9. In Java a method always returns a value.

10. In Java a code that is commented is not executed.

Solutions to the Quiz

1. TRUE.
2. TRUE.
3. TRUE.
4. TRUE.
5. TRUE.
6. TRUE.
7. TRUE.
8. TRUE.
9. FALSE.
10. TRUE.

Checklist

> You can move to the next chapter if you can do the following:
> - Create variables.
> - Combine variables.
> - Create a method.
> - Call a method.

> The solutions for the following challenges are included in the **resource pack** that you can download by following the instructions included in the section entitled "**Support and Resources for this Book**".

Challenge 1

Now that you have managed to complete this chapter and that you have gathered interesting skills, let's put these to the test. This particular challenge will get you to become more comfortable with methods. The solutions are included in the resource pack.

Create a method called **calculatePrice** that does the following:

- Take two parameters called **nbItems** and **unitPrice**.
- Multiply these two numbers and store the result in a variable called **finalPrice**.
- Return the value of the variable **finalPrice**.

Once the method has been created, call this method using two values of your choice and display the result returned by the method in the console window.

Challenge 2

Create a method that does the following:

- Asks the user for his/her first name.
- Asks the user for his/her first last name.

- Displays the full name (i.e., first name followed by a space, followed by the last name) in the console window.

- Once the method has been created, call this method.

2
Customized Data types & Structures

"Engineering is the closest thing to magic that exists in the world."

- Elon Musk

In this section you will discover how to work with customized methods and structures such as loops and conditional statements to optimize your code.

After completing this chapter, you will be able to:

- Work with Strings.
- Work with numbers.
- Work with loops and arrays.

WORKING WITH STRING VARIABLES

In the previous sections, we have learned how to declare and to manipulate variables such as numbers, and Strings. As we have seen earlier, it is possible to perform simple operations such as additions or concatenations with Strings. However, as we will see in this section, Java also offers useful built-in methods and attributes that make it possible to perform subtler operations on Strings and numbers. While there are many String methods in Java, we will focus, in this section, on some of the most useful and commonly employed methods and attributes to manipulate Strings.

So, let's look at some of these.

As we will see later, Strings are considered as objects (put simply, a variable that includes a collection of other variables and methods), with associated attributes (often called properties) and methods. These attributes and methods are accessible using what is called the dot notation, that is, by adding a dot after the name of the String, as we will see in the next examples.

So let's look at some attributes and methods for String variables.

length: length is a method that is available for all String variables and that provides the length of a String, which is the number of characters that it contains, as illustrated in the next code snippet.

```
String myName = "Patrick";
int numberOfLetters = myName.length();
System.out.println("There are " + numberOfLetters + " letters in " + myName);
```

In the previous code:

- We declare a String variable called **myName**.

- We then declare a new variable called **numberOfLetters** in which we will store the length of the String **myName**.

- We then display a message with the length of the String **myName**.

> Note that to access one of the attributes of a String, we use the **dot notation**, that is the name of the String followed by a dot followed by the name of the attribute or the method that we are looking for. This notation can be interpreted as the word "of" and it can be read from right to left. So, for example, **myString.length()** could be interpreted as the value returned by the method **length** <u>of</u> the variable **myString**.

IndexOf: this method returns the position where a character first appears in a String; it is useful when you would like to know if a String includes a specific character, and where this character is located within, as illustrated in the next code snippet.

```
String mySentence = "A sentence with the word Hello";
if (mySentence.indexOf("Hello") >= 0) System.out.println("Hello is part of the sentence");
else System.out.println("Hello is not included in the sentence");

if (mySentence.indexOf("Hi") >= 0) System.out.println("Hi is part of the sentence");
else System.out.println("Hi is not included in the sentence");
```

In the previous code:

- We declare a new String called **mySentence**.

- We check whether the word **Hello** appears in the sentence; since the first letter of the sentence starts at the index **0**, we know that if the word **Hello** appears from the index **0** onwards, that it is included in the sentence (since the index 0 refers to the start of the sentence); if that's the case, we display a message accordingly.

- We also check whether the word **Hi** appears in the sentence; since the first letter of the sentence starts at the index 0, we know that if the word **Hi** appears from the index 0 onwards, that it is included in the sentence.

- If that's the case, we then display a message accordingly.

You can now test this code by doing the following:

- Open the file **MyClass**.

- Comment the previous code in the method **main**.

- Add the following code to the method **main**.

Customized Data types & Structures

```
String mySentence = "A sentence with the word Hello";
if (mySentence.indexOf("Hello") >= 0) System.out.println("Hello is part of the sentence");
else System.out.println("Hello is not included in the sentence");


if (mySentence.indexOf("Hi") >= 0) System.out.println("Hi is part of the sentence");
else System.out.println("Hi is not included in the sentence");
```

- Please save your code and run the application; you should see the following messages in the console window.

```
Hello is part of the sentence
Hi is not included in the sentence
```

subString: In addition to locating a String within a String, Java also makes it possible to remove part of a String, and this can be performed using the method **SubString**, as illustrated in the next code snippet.

```
String mySentence = "This sentence is long and needs to be shorter";
String shorterSentence = mySentence.subString(0, 14);
System.out.println(shorterSentence);
```

In the previous code:

- We declare a new String variable called **mySentence**.

- We then remove part of this sentence starting at the first character (i.e., from the index 0) and ending at (and including) the 15th character (at the index 14).

- We then display the content of the new String.

You can add the above code to the **main** method for the file **MyClass** and see the result in the console window after running the application.

replace: Sometimes, it can be very useful to replace characters within a String, and this can be done by just looking for a String within a sentence or a paragraph, or by changing the case of a several letters in a sentence. This technique is useful when you are collecting information from the user, to ensure that some characters or words do not remain in the String entered by the user, or when you would like all the words in a sentence to be lower- or upper-case. The next code snippet illustrates how this can be done.

```
String mySentence = "This sentence is long and needs to be shorter";
String modifiedSentence = mySentence.replace("is long", "is way too long");
String upperCaseSentence = mySentence.toUpperCase();
String lowerCaseSentence = mySentence.toLowerCase();
```

In the previous code:

- We create a String called **mySentence**.

- We then replace the words **"is long"** by the words **"is way too long"** using the method **replace**, and we then save the result in the variable called **modifiedSentence**.

- In the next lines we successively convert all the letters in the variable **mySentence** to upper-case (using the method **toUpperCase**) or to lower-case (using the method **toLowerCase**).

We could test these methods ourselves, by doing the following:

- Open the file **MyClass** in your code editor.

- Comment the previous code located in the **main** method

- Add the following code to the **main** method.

Customized Data types & Structures

```
String mySentence = "This sentence is long and needs to be
shorter";
String shorterSentence = mySentence.subString(0, 14);
System.out.println(shorterSentence);
String modifiedSentence = mySentence.replace("is long", "is way
too long");
System.out.println(modifiedSentence);
String upperCaseSentence = mySentence.toUpperCase();
System.out.println("Upper Case: " + upperCaseSentence);
String lowerCaseSentence = mySentence.toLowerCase();
System.out.println("Lower Case: " + lowerCaseSentence);
```

In the previous code, as we have seen earlier, we perform several operations on the String called **mySentence** and we then display the result in the console window.

Please save the code, refresh the corresponding web browser page, and you should see the following messages in the console window.

```
This sentence is way too long and needs to be shorter
Upper Case: THIS SENTENCE IS LONG AND NEEDS TO BE SHORTER
Lower Case: this sentence is long and needs to be shorter
```

While we have covered some of the most common String methods here, you can see a full list of Java String methods on the official website:

https://docs.oracle.com/Javase/9/docs/api/Java/lang/String.html

WORKING WITH NUMBER VARIABLES

As you can see, built-in methods can be very useful when it comes to working with Strings. Thankfully, built-in methods also exist for numbers so that they can be manipulated accordingly, sometimes through mathematical calculations.

So, let's look at some very useful built-in attributes and methods that can be used with numbers.

These attributes (or properties) and methods can help to perform conversions between different types of variables, as follows:

- **toString**: this method converts a number to a String.

- **Integer.ParseInt**: this method converts a String to an integer (i.e., a number with no decimals).

- **Float.parseFloat**: this method converts a String to a float (i.e., to a number with decimals).

Java also includes methods and classes that make it possible to perform advanced mathematical calculations, including:

- **Math.random**: Returns a random number.

- **Math.pow (x,y)**: returns the value of x to the power of y.

- **Math.ceil (x)**: returns the value of x rounded-up to its nearest integer.

- **Math.floor (x)**: returns the value of x rounded-down to its nearest integer.

- **Math.sin (x)**: returns the sine of the angle x.

- **Math.min (x, y):** returns the lowest number in the list of arguments.

- **Math.max (x, y)**: returns the highest number in the list of arguments.

Let's experiment with some of these:

- Please open the file called **MyClass**.

- Comment the previous code in the **main** class.

- Add the following code to the **main** method:

[75]

Customized Data types & Structures

```
double randomNumber= Math.random();

System.out.println("Random Number: "+randomNumber);

if (randomNumber < 0.7) System.out.println("there was a 70% chance for this message to be displayed");

else System.out.println("there was a 30% chance for this message to be displayed");
```

In the previous code:

- We create a variable **randomNumber** that will store a random number that will range between 0 and .99.

- We display the value of the variable **randomNumber**.

- We then test whether this random number is less than **0.7**.

- In both cases (i.e., whether it is greater than or less than 0.7) we display a message in the console window accordingly.

Please save your code and run the application. You should see a message displayed in the console window for which the content will vary depending on the random number generated.

Next, we could experiment with some Maths methods, as follows:

- Please comment the code currently used in the **main** method.

- Add the following code to the **main** method and run your application; you should see the two messages displaying the smallest of the first two numbers and the greatest of the two other numbers as illustrated in the next figure.

```
int minimum = Math.min(2, 3);

System.out.println("The smallest number between 2 and 3 is " + minimum);


int maximum= Math.max(100, 900);

System.out.println("The greatest number between 100 and 900 is " + maximum);
```

Again, we have only looked at common methods here; for a list of all the Maths methods you can look at the official documentation:

https://docs.oracle.com/Javase/8/docs/api/Java/lang/Math.html

SWITCH STATEMENTS

If you have understood the concept of conditional statements in the previous sections, then this section should be pretty much straight forward. Switch statements are a variation on the if/else statements that we have seen earlier. The idea behind the switch statements is that, depending on the value of a specific variable, we will switch to a portion of the code and perform one or several actions accordingly. The variable considered for the switch structure is usually a **number**. Let's look at a simple example:

```java
int choice = 1;
switch (choice)
{
    case 1:
        System.out.println ("you chose 1");
        break;
    case 2:
        System.out.println ("you chose 2");
        break;
    case 3:
        System.out.println ("you chose 3");
        break;
    default:
        System.out.println ("Default option");
        break;
}
System.out.println ("We have exited the switch structure");
```

In the previous code:

- We declare the variable called **choice** as an **integer**, and we then initialize it to **1**.

- We then create a **switch** structure whereby, depending on the value of the variable **choice**, the program will switch to the relevant section (i.e., the portion of code starting with **case 1:**, **case 2:**, etc.). Note that in our code, we look for the values **1**, **2** or **3**. However, if the variable **choice** is not equal to 1 or 2 or 3, the program

Customized Data types & Structures

will go to the section called **default**. This is because this section is executed if none of the other possible conditions (i.e., choice=1, choice=2, or choice=3) have been fulfilled.

> Note that each choice or branch starts with the keyword **case** and ends with the keyword **break**. The **break** keyword is there to specify that after executing the commands included in a specific branch (or the current choice), the program should exit the switch structure. Without any break statement, we will remain in the switch structure and the next line of code would be executed.

So let's consider the previous example and see how this would work in practice. In our case, the variable **choice** is set to **1**, so we will enter the **switch** structure, and then look for the section that deals with a value of **1** for the variable **choice**. This will be the section that starts with **case 1:**. Then the command **System.out.println ("you chose 1");** will be executed, followed by the command **break**, indicating that we should exit the switch structure; finally, the command **System.out.println ("We have exited the switch structure")** will be executed.

Switch structures are very useful to structure your code and when dealing with mutually exclusive choices (i.e., only one of the choices can be selected) based on an integer value, especially in the case of menus. In addition, switch structures make for cleaner and easily understandable code.

So, let's experiment with the switch structure:

- Please open the file **MyClass**.
- Comment any previous code present in the **main** method.
- Add the following code to the **main** method:

```
System.out.println("Please pick your choice 1-3");
Scanner sc= new Scanner (System.in);
String answer= sc.nextLine();
int choice = Integer.parseInt(answer);
switch (choice)
{
    case 1:
        System.out.println("you chose 1");
        break;
    case 2:
        System.out.println("you chose 2");
        break;
    case 3:
        System.out.println("you chose 3");
        break;
    default:
        System.out.println("Default option");
        break;
}
System.out.println("We have exited the switch structure");
```

In the previous code:

- We ask the user to enter a choice between **1** and **3**.
- We convert this choice to a number.
- We then display a corresponding message using a switch structure.
- After exiting the switch structure, we display another message.

You can now save your code and run the application, and you should see the following message:

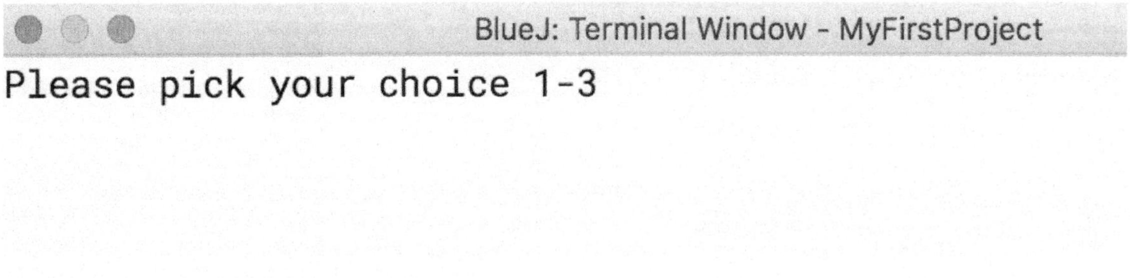

Customized Data types & Structures

```
BlueJ: Terminal Window - MyFirstProject
Please pick your choice 1-3
```

Figure 2-1: Asking for a number

Once you enter a number and press **Enter**, a message similar to the following should be displayed in the console window.

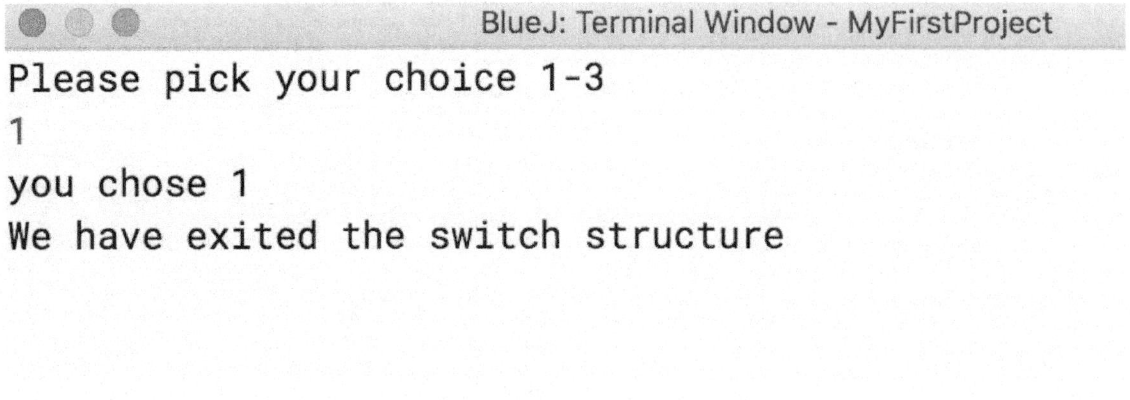

```
BlueJ: Terminal Window - MyFirstProject
Please pick your choice 1-3
1
you chose 1
We have exited the switch structure
```

Figure 2-2: Displaying the choice in the console window

SINGLE-DIMENSIONAL ARRAYS

You can optimize your code with arrays, as they make it easier to apply common features and similar behaviors to a wide range of data. When you use arrays, you can manage to declare less variables (for variables storing the same type of information) and to also access them more easily. You can create either single-dimensional arrays or multi-dimensional arrays.

Let's look at the simplest form of arrays: **single-dimensional arrays**. For this concept, we can take the analogy of a group of 10 people who all have a name. If we wanted to store this information using a String variable, we would need to declare (and to set) ten different variables, as illustrated in the next code snippet.

```
String name1;String name2; ......
```

While this code is perfectly fine, it would be great to store this information in only one variable instead. For this purpose, we could use an array. An array is comparable to a list of items that we can access using an index. This index usually starts at 0 for the first element in the array.

So let's see how we store the names with an array.

- First we could declare the array as follows:

```
String [] names;
```

You will probably notice the syntax **dataType [] nameOfTheArray**. The opening and closing square brackets are used to specify that we declare an **array** that will include String values.

- Then we could initialize the array as follows:

```
names = new String [10];
```

In the previous code, we just specify that our new array, called **names**, will include 10 String variables.

- We can then store information in this array as described in the next code snippet.

Customized Data types & Structures

```
names [0] = "Paul";
names [1] = "Mary";
...
names [9] = "Pat";
```

In the previous code, we store the name **Paul** as the first element in the array (remember the index starts at 0); we store the second element (with the index 1) as **Mary**, as well as the last element (with the index 9), **Pat**.

> Note that for an array of size **n**, **the index of the first element is 0** and **the index of the last element is n-1**. So for an array of size 10, the index for the first element is 0, and the index of the last element is 9 (i.e., 10-1).

If you were to use arrays of integers or floats, or any other type of data, the process would be similar, as illustrated in the next code snippet.

```
int [] arrayOfInts; arrayOfInts [0] = 1;
float [] arrayOfFloats;arrayOfFloats[0]=2.4f;
```

Now, one of the cool things that you can do with arrays is that you can initialize your array in one line, saving you the headaches of writing 10 lines of code if you have 10 items in your array, as illustrated in the next example.

```
String [] names = new String [10] {"Paul","Mary","John","Mark",
"Eva","Pat","Sinead","Elma","Flaithri", "Eleanor"};
```

This is very handy, as you will see in the next chapters, and this should definitely save you a lot of time coding.

To illustrate the concept of arrays, we could create a very simple quiz where the user is asked several questions, and his/her answers are compared to the correct answers.

- Please open the file **MyClass**

- Add the following method. This should be done outside of any other method. For example, after the closing curly bracket for the **main** method.

```java
public static void arrayExample()
{
    String[] questions = { "What is 2+2", "What is 4+2", "What is 4+5"};
    int[] correctAnswers = { 4, 6, 9 };
    for (int i = 0; i < 3; i++)
    {
        System.out.println(questions[i]);
        Scanner sc= new Scanner (System.in);
        int answer= sc.nextInt();
        if (answer == correctAnswers[i])
        {
            System.out.println("Well done!");
        }
        else System.out.println("Sorry wrong answer");
    }
}
```

In the previous code:

- We declare an array called **questions**, and we define its content. The array consists of three Strings that relate to the questions of the quiz.

- We then define a new array called **correctAnswers** and we define its content. The array consists of the three solutions to the quiz.

- We create a loop; the idea is to go through the three questions of the quiz, to collect the answers from the user, and to check if they are correct.

- The first time we go through the loop, **i = 0**; we use the String included in **question [0]** for the question; that is, the text "**what is 2 + 2**"; we then record the answer, convert it to a number, and save it in the variable called **answer**; following this, we compare the answer from the user to the correct answer, that is **corretAnswer[0]** (which is 6) and display a message accordingly.

Finally, we just need to call this method doing the following:

- Please comment all the code in the function **main**.

Customized Data types & Structures

- Add this code in the **main** method instead:

```
arrayExample();
```

You can now save your code, compile it, and run the application. You should see that if you enter the correct answer to the first question (i.e., 4), a message should display the text "**Well done!**'.

We could even jazz-up this quiz by adding the following:

- The question number.
- The total number of correct answers.
- The total number of incorrect answers.

So let's proceed with these changes.

- Please modify the code for the function **arrayExample** as follows (new code in bold):

```java
String[] questions = { "What is 2+2", "What is 4+2", "What is 4+5"};
    int[] correctAnswers = { 4, 6, 9 };

    int score = 0;
    for (int i = 0; i < 3; i++)
    {
        System.out.println("Question "+(i+1)+": "+ questions[i]);
        Scanner sc= new Scanner (System.in);
        int answer= sc.nextInt();
        if (answer == correctAnswers[i])
        {
            System.out.println("Well done!");
            score++;
        }
        else System.out.println("Sorry wrong answer");
    }
    System.out.println("You answered " + score + " questions correctly");
```

Customized Data types & Structures

In the previous code:

- We declare a variable called **score** that will be used to track the score.

- When asking a new question to the user, we add the String "**Question**" followed by **i+1** to display the question number; so when **i = 0** we display the label "**Question 1**", and so forth.

- Whenever a correct answer has been given, we increase the score by one.

- When all answers have been provided (i.e., when we are outside the loop) we display the number of correct questions.

You can now save your code and run the application; you should see that each question includes a label with the question number, as illustrated in the next figure.

```
Question 0 :What is 2+2
4
Well done!
Question 1 :What is 4+2
6
Well done!
Question 2 :What is 4+5
9
Well done!
You answered 3 questions correctly
```

You should also see that the score is provided at the end of the quiz (i.e., after the last question has been answered).

> One of the other interesting aspects of arrays is that, by using a loop, you can write a single line of code to access all the items in this array, and hence, write more efficient code.

You can also use built-in functions (i.e., methods) to manage your arrays and to perform actions such as adding elements, removing elements, or even sorting the array.

Let's look at the **sort** function that is used in the next code snippet:

```
import Java.util.Arrays;
...
String[] test = { "Noemy", "Alan", "John" };
System.out.println("First Element before sort: " + test[0]);
Arrays.sort(test);
System.out.println("First Element after sort: " + test[0]);
```

In the previous code:

- We include a line at the beginning of the file that imports the class called **Arrays** that can then be used to sort our array.
- We declare an array made of three names, called **test**.
- We display the first element of the array before it is sorted.
- We sort the array using the **sort** function.
- We display the first element of the array before it is sorted.
- The result of the code snippet is illustrated in the next figure.

```
First Element before sort: Noemy
First Element after sort: Alan
```

Figure 2-3: Sorting the array

In our previous example, the elements of the array are sorted based on the first letter of each name. If this array included numbers instead, then they would have been sorted by increasing number, as per the next example.

```
int[] test = {8,6,9,4,7};
System.out.println("First Element before sort: " + test[0]);
Arrays.sort(test);
System.out.println("First Element after sort: " + test[0]);
```

In the previous code, we create an array of numbers and we display its content before and after it has been sorted. The result is illustrated in the next figure.

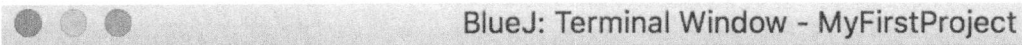

```
First Element before sort: 8
First Element after sort: 4
```

Figure 2-4: Sorting an array of numbers

You can, if you wish, use the previous code to sort numerical arrays and check that you obtain the same result.

For a full list of array functions, please see the official documentation here:

https://docs.oracle.com/Javase/8/docs/api/Java/util/Arrays.html

MULTI-DIMENSIONAL ARRAYS

Now that we have looked into single-dimensional arrays, let's look at multidimensional arrays, which can also be very useful when storing information. This type of array (i.e., multidimensional arrays) can be compared to a building with several floors, each with several apartments. So let's say that we would like to store the number of tenants for each apartment. We would, in this case, create variables that would store this number for each of these apartments.

The first solution would be to create variables that store the number of tenants for each of these apartments with a variable that makes a reference to the floor and the number of the apartment. For example, the variable **ap0_1** could be defined to store the number of tenants in the first apartment on the ground floor, **ap0_2**, could be defined to store the number of tenants in the second apartment on the ground floor, **ap1_1** could be defined to store the number of tenants in the second apartment on the first floor, and **ap1_2**, could be defined to store the number of tenants in the third apartment on the first floor. So in term of coding, we could have the following:

```
int ap0_1 = 0;
int ap0_2 = 0;
…
```

However, we could also use arrays in this case, to make our code more efficient, as illustrated in the next code snippet:

```
int [][] apArray = new int [10][10];
apArray [0][1] = 0;
apArray [0][2] = 0;
System.out.println(apArray[0][1]);
```

In the previous code:

- We declare our array.

- The code **int [][]** corresponds to a two-dimensional array of integers; in other words, we state that any element in this array will be defined and accessed based on two parameters: the floor level and the number of this apartment on that level.

- We also specify a size (or maximum) for each of these parameters. The maximum number of floors (or level) will be 10, and the maximum number of apartment per floor will be 10. So, for this example we can define 10 levels, from level 0 to

Customized Data types & Structures

level 9 (i.e., 10 levels), and for each of these levels we can also define 10 apartments from apartment 0 to apartment 9.

- The last line of code prints the value of the first element of the array in the **console** window.

> One of the other interesting things with arrays is that, by using a loop, you can write a single line of code to access all the items in this array, and hence, write more efficient code.

LOOPS

There are times when you have to perform repetitive tasks as a programmer; many times, these can be fast-forwarded using loops which are structures that will perform the same actions repetitively based on a condition. So, the process is usually as follows when using loops:

- Start the loop.
- Perform actions.
- Check for a condition.
- Exit the loop if the condition is fulfilled or keep looping otherwise.

Sometimes the condition is tested at the start of the loop, some other times it is tested at the end of the loop. As we will see in the next paragraph, this will be the case for the **while** and **do-while** loop structures, respectively.

Let's look at the following example that is using a **while** loop.

```
int counter = 0;
while (counter <=10)
{
    counter++;
}
```

In the previous code:

- We declare the variable called **counter** and set its value to **0**.
- We then create a loop that starts with the keyword **while** and for which the content (which is what is to be executed while we are looping) is delimited by opening and closing curly brackets.
- We set the condition to remain in this loop (i.e., **counter <=10**). So we will remain in this loop as long as the variable counter is **less than or equal to 10**.
- Every time we go through the loop, we increase the value of the variable **counter** by **1**.

So effectively:

- The first time we go through the loop: the variable **counter** is increased to **1**; we reach the end of the loop; we go back to the start of the loop and check if the variable **counter** is less or equal to **10**; this is true in this case because **counter** equals 1.

- The second time we go through the loop: the variable **counter** is increased to **2**; we reach the end of the loop; we go back to the start of the loop and check if the variable **counter** is less or equal to 10; this is true in this case because **counter** equals **2**.

- ...

- The 11th time we go through the loop: the variable **counter** is increased to **11**; we reach the end of the loop; we go back to the start of the loop and check if the variable **counter** is less or equal to 10; this is now false as **counter** now equals **11**. As a result, we exit the loop.

So, as you can see, using a loop, we have managed to increment the value of the variable **counter** iteratively, from 0 to 11, but using less code than would be needed otherwise.

Now, we could create a slightly modified version of this loop, using a **do-while** loop structure instead, as illustrated in the next example:

```
int counter = 0;
do
{
    counter++;
} while (counter <=10);
```

In the previous example, you may spot two differences, compared to the previous code:

- The **while** keyword is now at the end of the loop. So the condition will be tested (or assessed) at the end of the loop.

- A **do** keyword is now featured at the start of the loop.

So here, we execute statements first and then check for the condition at the end of the loop.

Another variation of the code could be as follows:

```
for (int counter = 0; counter <=10; counter ++)
{
     System.out.println ("Counter = " + counter);
}
```

In the previous code:

- We declare a loop in a slightly different way: we state that we will use an integer variable called **counter** that will go from 0 to 10.

- This variable **counter** will be incremented by **1** every time we go through the loop.

- We remain in the loop as long as the variable **counter** is less than or equal to 10.

- The test for the condition, in this case, is performed at the start of the loop.

Loops are very useful to perform repetitive actions for a finite number of objects, or to perform what is usually referred as recursive actions. For example, you could use loops to go through an array of 100 items. As a result, using loops will definitely save you some code and time when you use them.

So we could use a loop structure to improve the previous code to keep asking the user to enter a number as long as his/her choice is less than 1 or greater than 3, or if the data entered is not a number.

Let's just do that:

- Please open the file **MyClass**

- Add the following method to the file **MyClass** as follows:

```
public static void selectChoice()
{
    int myChoice = 0;
    do
    {
        System.out.println("Please enter your choice 1- 3");
        Scanner sc= new Scanner (System.in);
        myChoice= sc.nextInt();
    } while (myChoice < 1 || myChoice > 3);
    System.out.println("Thank you");
}
```

In the previous code:

- We create a new method called **selectChoice**.
- We create a variable called **myChoice** that will be used to record the user's choice.
- We create a **do-while** loop.
- We record and check the user's choice.
- We loop as long as the number entered by the user is **less than 1 or greater than 3**.

You can now comment your code in the method **main**, and then add the following code to the same method, so that we can call the method **selectChoice** from there:

```
selectChoice();
```

You can now save the file called **MyClass**, and run the application; the system will ask you for a number between 1 and 3, and it will keep doing so as long as the number that you enter is less than **1** or greater than **3**, as illustrated in the next figure.

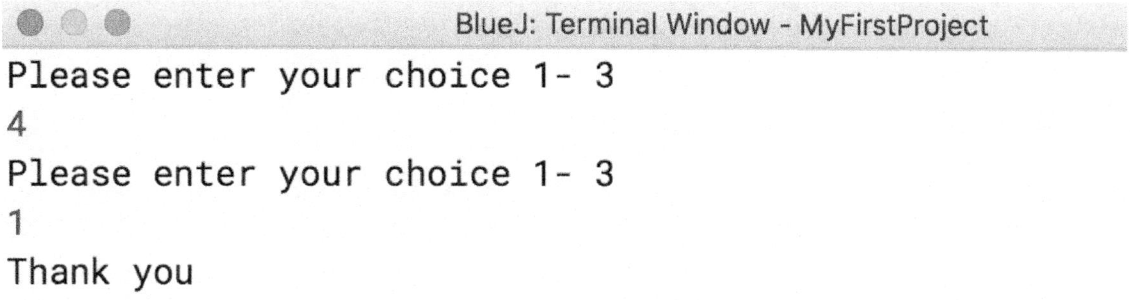

```
BlueJ: Terminal Window - MyFirstProject
Please enter your choice 1- 3
4
Please enter your choice 1- 3
1
Thank you
```

Figure 2-5: Looping until the correct information is provided

CONSTANTS

So far, we have looked at variables and how you can store and access them seamlessly in your code. The assumption then was that a value may change over time, and that this value would be stored in a variable accordingly. However, there may be times when you know that a value will remain constant throughout your application. For example, you may want to define labels that refer to values that should not change over time, and in this case, you could use constants.

Let's see how this works: let's say that the user has three choices in the first menu of the application, that we will call **0**, **1**, and **2**. Let's assume that you would like an easy way to remember these values so that you can process the corresponding choices. Let's look at the following code that illustrates this idea:

```
int userChoice = 2;
if (userChoice == 0) System.out.println("you have decided to restart");

if (userChoice == 1) System.out.println("you have decided to stop the application");

if (userChoice == 2) System.out.println("you have decided to pause the application");
```

In the previous code:

- The variable **userChoice** is an integer and is set to **2**.

- We then check the value of the variable **userChoice** and print a message accordingly in the console window.

Now, as you add more code to your application, you may or may not remember that the value **0** corresponds to restarting the application; the same applies to the other two values defined previously. So instead, we could use constants to make it easier to remember (and to use) these values. Let's see how the previous example can be modified to employ constants instead.

```java
public class MyClass
{
    public static int myMemberVariable;
    public static final int CHOICE_RESTART = 0;
    public static final int CHOICE_STOP = 1;
    public static final int CHOICE_PAUSE = 2;
    public static void testConstants()
    {


        int userChoice = CHOICE_RESTART;
        if (userChoice == CHOICE_RESTART) System.out.println("you have decided to restart");
        if (userChoice == CHOICE_STOP) System.out.println("you have decided to stop the application");
        if (userChoice == CHOICE_PAUSE) System.out.println("you have decided to pause the application");


    }
```

In the previous code:

- We declare three **constant** variables: **CHOICE_RESTART**, **CHOICE_STOP** and **CHOICE_PAUSE**.

Note that it is common practice to use upper-case letters for constants, so that they stand out.

- These variables are then used to check the choice made by the user.
- To declare a constant variable, we use the keywords **static** and **final**; the keyword **final** means that the variable cannot be reassigned and the keyword **static** means that the value for this variable is accessible from each instance of the class or without the class being instantiated.

You can now test this feature by doing the following:

- Please add the following code at the beginning of the class (new code in bold):

Customized Data types & Structures

```
public class MyClass
{
    public static int myMemberVariable;
    public static final int CHOICE_RESTART = 0;
    public static final int CHOICE_STOP = 1;
    public static final int CHOICE_PAUSE = 2;
```

- Please add the following method to the file **MyClass**.

```
public static void useConstants()
{
    int userChoice = CHOICE_RESTART;
    if (userChoice == CHOICE_RESTART) System.out.println("you have decided to restart");
    if (userChoice == CHOICE_STOP) System.out.println("you have decided to stop the application");
    if (userChoice == CHOICE_PAUSE) System.out.println("you have decided to pause the application");

}
```

You can then comment the code in the **main** method and add the following line in the same method, so that we call the method **useConstants** from there.

```
useConstants();
```

After saving your code, and launching the application, you should see a message saying **"You have decided to restart"**.

In the next example, we use a constant to calculate a tax rate; this is a good practice as the same value will be used across the program with no or little room for errors when it comes to using the exact same tax rate across your program.

```
public static final float VAT_RATE = 0.21f;
...
float priceBeforeVat = 23.0f;
float priceAfterVat = priceBeforeVat * VAT_RATE;
```

In the previous code:

- We declare a **constant float** variable for the vat rate.
- We declare a **float** variable for the item's price before tax.
- We calculate the item's price after adding the tax.

> It is a very good coding practice to use constants for values that don't change across your program. Using constants makes your code more readable, it saves work when you need to change a value in your code, and it also decreases possible occurrences of errors (e.g., for calculations).

LEVEL ROUNDUP

Summary

In this chapter, we have managed to use customized structured such as loops, or switch statements. We also worked with Strings and numbers and discovered some very interesting methods to manipulate these. We also used arrays and discovered how to create and sort elements within an array. Next, we used loops to be able to read arrays and to create a simple quiz. Finally, we used constants. So we have covered some significant ground here from no knowledge of Java to creating your first application: well done!

Quiz

It is now time to test your knowledge. Please specify whether the following statements are TRUE or FALSE. The answers are available on the next page.

1. The method **indexOf**: this method returns the position where a character first appears in a String.

2. The method **replace**, replaces part of an existing String.

3. **Math.floor (x)**: returns the value of x rounded-up to its nearest integer.

4. The command **System.out.println** displays information in the *Console* window.

5. The objects **Scanner** record information entered by the user in the *Console* window.

6. A switch statement is a type of conditional statement.

7. The following code declares a single-dimensional array of String variables.

```
String [String] myArray;
```

8. The following code declares a single-dimensional array of int variables.

```
int [] myArray = {1,3,4,5,7};
```

9. The following code creates a loop that will go from 0 to 9.

```
for (int i = 0; i < 10; i++){}
```

10. The following code will create a constant of type int.

```
public static final int CHOICE_RESTART = 0;
```

Solutions to the Quiz

1. TRUE.
2. TRUE.
3. FALSE (its rounded-down).
4. TRUE.
5. TRUE.
6. TRUE.
7. FALSE; it should be as follows:

```
String [] myArray;
```

8. TRUE
9. TRUE.
10. TRUE.

Checklist

You can move to the next chapter if you can do the following:

- Create arrays.
- Create loops.
- Use some of the String methods (e.g., subString or replace).
- Call a method.

The solution for the following challenge is included in the **resource pack** that you can download by following the instructions included in the section entitled "**Support and Resources for this Book**".

Challenge 1

Now that you have managed to complete this chapter and that you have gathered interesting skills, let's put these to the test. This particular challenge will get you to become more comfortable with methods. The solutions are included in the resource pack.

Create a method called **myQuiz** that does the following:

- Includes 10 questions and answers in respective arrays.
- Uses a loop to ask the question.
- Records the user's answer.
- Records the score (+1 for each correct answer).
- Provides feedback every time an answer is entered ("Correct" or "Incorrect").
- Provides the final score at the end of the 10 questions.
- Call this method from the **main** method.

3
OBJECT-ORIENTED PROGRAMMING & CLASSES

"When I do something, it is all about self-discovery. I want to learn and discover my own limits."

- Larry Ellison

In this section you will discover how to leverage the Object-Oriented features of Java.

After completing this chapter, you will be able to:

- Understand the concepts of classes and objects.
- Create your own class.
- Understand and use the concepts of inheritance, polymorphisms and encapsulation.

Why use Object-Oriented Programming

So far, you have managed to learn and to understand some very interesting programming concepts such as variables and functions (or methods) as well as control structures such as loops and conditional statements. So, even without using object-oriented programming, you could at this stage create some very interesting programmes very easily.

However, what if you wanted to build several programmes that re-use some of the code that you have already created? What if you would prefer not to re-invent the wheel and to re-use components that you have already created for a previous programme?

In many cases, if you stick to a procedural-oriented programme that just consists of functions (methods) and variables, and control structures, this would be very difficult. For example, if you wanted to reuse a function that you have already created in a different programme, you would need to manually copy/paste it into the new programme.

This because functions, when written in non-Object-Oriented environment, are not designed to be reusable in a different context without actually opening the previous code and copy/pasting it in a different programme. In addition, the use of functions, variables and control structures may not make it possible to model (and consequently solve) a real-life problem, because procedural approaches differentiate between data and functions and don't use a high-level abstraction. In other words: it is difficult to understand how the code relates to what we are trying to model, just by looking at it.

For example, if you want to create a programme that tries to model the way soccer players interact on the field, you would typical create functions to move the player and the ball, but the structure of the programme may be difficult to understand. Functions may exist, but it may difficult to understand how they relate to the players or the ball. In addition, reusing some of this code to create another game, but this time a basketball game, may mean that most of it would need to be rewritten or copy/pasted.

All in all, using a procedural approach can make your code less maintainable, less reusable, and overall prone to duplication, hence, more time-consuming.

On the other hand, OOP programmes are designed to palliate some of the issues found in procedural programming, that is: data and associated algorithms (i.e., methods) are "encapsulated" within a class, and are hence reusable. In addition, the use of classes and objects makes it possible to model the issue that you are trying to solve based on the what you are trying to model rather than your own programme logic. For example, if you want to create a game of soccer and then a game of basket-ball, you can create classes that will be reusable and employed in both games, to model the entities involved in the game with meaningful names and associated data and methods; for example, you could create a classes such as Ball, Player, Field, Rules, etc. Using the power of inheritance, as we will see later, you will also be able to create more specific behaviors depending on the game that you are developing, all resulting in code that can be reused across programmes, and that is easier to understand as the classes provide a virtual, and more understandable representation of the entities for each type of game.

Classes

When coding in Java, you will be creating applications that are either classes or that use built-in classes. So what is a class?

As we have seen earlier, Java is an Object-Oriented Programming (OOP) language. Put simply, a Java programme will consist of a collection of objects that interact amongst themselves. Each object has one or more attributes, and it is possible to perform actions on these objects using what are called methods. In addition, objects that share the same properties are said to belong to the same **class**. The idea here is that we will encapsulate both the data and the algorithm (e.g., methods) related to an entity in one class.

For example, we could take the analogy of a bike. There are bikes of all shapes and colors; however, they share common features. For example, they all have a specific number of wheels (e.g., one, two or three) or a speed; they can have a color, and actions can be performed on these bikes (e.g., accelerate, turn right, turn left, etc.).

So in object-oriented programming, to group all data and algorithms associated to a bike, we could create a class called **Bike**, that includes variables such as **speed** or **color** (these would be referred as member variables or attributes), and algorithms or methods that can be applied to bikes, such as accelerate a method called **accelerate**.

Once this class has been created, it could be reused in different programme; for example, a bike race, or a bike shop, or a game where the player explore the environment with a bike. As you see, creating a class called Bike makes the code reusable. The class is declared once and it can then be used several times. In addition, we can make modifications to the class called Bike and these changes will be propagated to all the games that use this class. So this would certainly save us significant time.

So if we were to define a common type, we could define a class called **Bike** and for this class define several member variables and attributes that would make it possible to define and perform actions on the objects of type **Bike**.

This is, obviously, a simplified explanation of classes and objects, but it should give you a clearer idea of the concept of object-oriented programming if you are new to it, and explain how useful it is to use classes rather than just variables, functions, and control structures.

DEFINING A CLASS

Now that we have a clearer idea of what a class is, let's see how we could define a class. So let's look at the following example.

```
public class Bike
{
    private float speed;
    private int color;

    public void accelerate()
    {
        speed++;
    }
    public void turnRight()
    {
    }
    private void calculateDistance()
    {
    }
}
```

In the previous code, we have defined a class, called **Bike**, that includes two member variables (**speed** and **color**) as well as two member methods (**accelerate** and **turnRight**). So again here we encapsulate all the data and algorithms linked to a bike in one class. This way, it is easier to see what can be done with a bike; it also makes our code more modular. Let's look at the class a little closer; you may notice a few things:

- The name of the class is preceded by the keywords **public class**; in OOP terms, the keyword **public** is called an **access modifier** and it defines how (and from where) this class may be accessed and used. In Java there are four types of access modifiers, including **public** (no restrictions), **protected** (access limited to the containing class, classes from the same package – a grouping of files -, and subclasses from other packages), **default** (this this the default mode if no access modifier is specified; in this case, access is limited to the containing class and classes from the same package) and **private** (access only from the containing class or type). So in our case, we should be to use this class anywhere in our programme.

- The names of all variables are preceded by their type (i.e., **int**), and the keyword **public**: this means that these integer variables will be accessible throughout our application (i.e., from outside the class if need be).m

- Some of the names of the methods are preceded by the keywords **public void** (e.g., for the methods **accelerate** or **turnRight**): the **void** keyword means that the method does not return any data, while the keyword **public** means that the method will be accessible throughout our application.

- Some of the names of the methods are preceded by the keywords **private void** (e.g., for the method **calculateDistance**): the **void** keyword means that the method does not return any data, while the keyword **private** means that the method will be accessible only from the containing type (i.e., **Bike**).

So by defining the class **Bike**, we effectively define a template that can be used later on to create bikes. Once new bikes are created, it will be possible to modify their properties/ (or attributes). Again, this class can be used in any programme, so it is totally reusable; it just needs to be defined once, and then used to create new bikes. Again, all the data and algorithms related to a bike is encapsulated in the class Bike. Looking at the class, it is easy to understand how the data and the algorithms related to each other, and it is consequently easier to maintain the code.

Object-Oriented Programming & Classes

ACCESSING CLASS MEMBERS AND VARIABLES

Once a class has been defined, it is great to be able to access its member variables and methods. In Java (as for other object-oriented programming languages), this can be done using the **dot notation**.

> The dot notation refers to **object-oriented programming**. Using dots, you can access properties and/or methods related to a particular object.

Once a class has been defined, objects based on this class can be created. For example, if we were to create a new **Bike** object, based on the code that we have seen above, the following code could be used in the file **MyClass**, within the **main** method.

```
Bike myBike = new Bike();
```

This code will create (or instantiate) an object based on the "template" **Bike**. You may notice the syntax:

```
dataType variable = new dataType()
```

By default, this new object will include all the member variables and methods defined earlier in the class **Bike**. So it will have a color and a speed, and we should also be able to access its **accelerate** and **turnRight** methods.

So using the Object-Oriented approach, we can define a template for an object and use this template to create a new object that includes all the data and methods (algorithm) necessary to manage or modify this object.

So how can this be done?

Let's look at the next code snippet that shows how we can access these.

```
Bike b = new Bike();
b.accelerate();
```

In the previous code:

- The new bike **myBike** is created.

- The speed is then increased after calling the **accelerate** method. This method can be called using the dot notation because it is **public**.

- Note that to call an object's method we use the dot notation.

> When defining member variables and methods, it is usually good practice to restrict the access to member variables (e.g., to the **private** type) and to define public methods with no or less strict restrictions (e.g., **public**) that provide access to these variables. These methods are often referred to as **getters** and **setters** because you can get or set the value of member variables from them.

To illustrate this concept, let's look at the following code:

```
public class Bike
{
    private float speed;
    private int color;
    public void accelerate()
    {
        speed++;
    }
    public void turnRight()
    {
    }
    private void claculateDistance()
    {
    }
    public void setSpeed(float newSpeed)
    {
        speed = newSpeed;
    }
    public float getSpeed()
    {
        return (speed);
    }
}
```

In the previous code, we have declared two new methods: **setSpeed** and **getSpeed**.

Object-Oriented Programming & Classes

- For **setSpeed**: the type is **void** as this method does not return any information, and its access is set to **public**, so that it can be accessed with no restrictions.

- For **getSpeed**: the type is **float** as this method returns the speed, which type is float. Its access is set to **public**, so that it can be accessed with no restrictions.

So, let's create our own class and use some of these concepts:

- From the main window in BlueJ, please select the option **Edit | New Class** from the top menu.

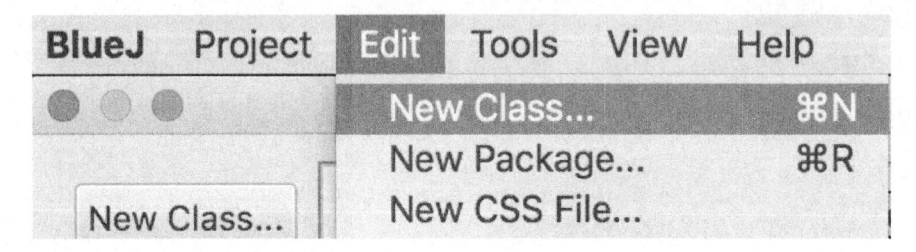

Figure 3-1: Creating a new class

- In the new window, enter the word **Bike** in the field labelled "**Class Name**".

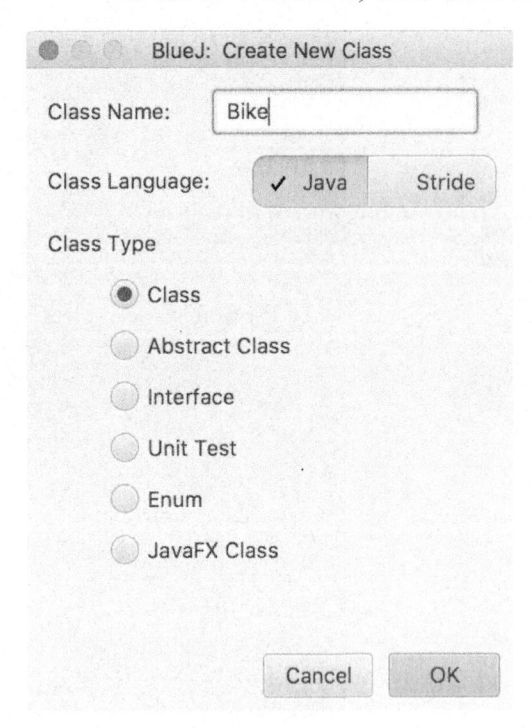

Figure 3-2: Creating a new class

[112]

- Once this is done, please click on the button labelled "**OK**".
- This will create a new class called **Bike** in the project window. As per the next figure.

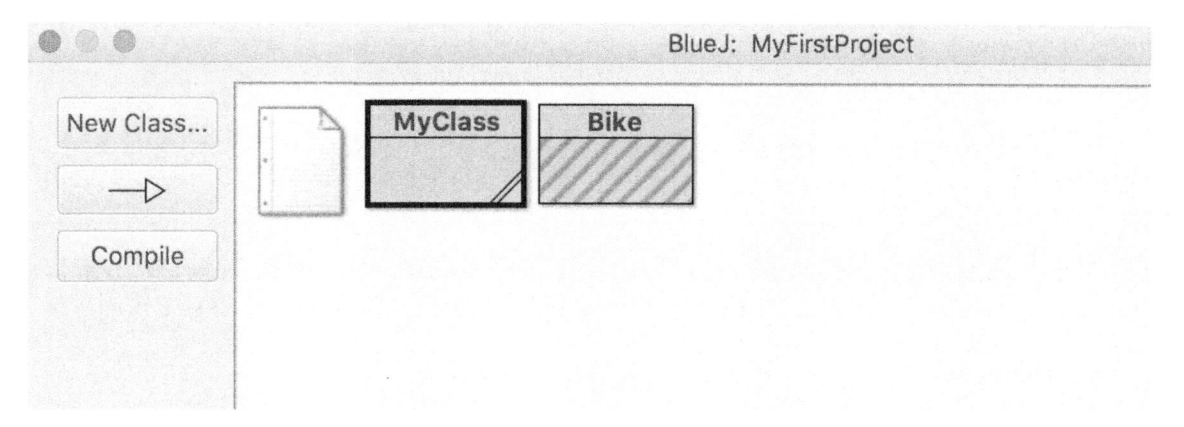

Figure 3-3: Creating the new class Bike

Once this is done, you can double click on the icon labelled "**Bike**" in the main window, this should open the content of the class **Bike** with some default code.

You can then delete all the code in this file and replace it with the following.

```
public class Bike
{
    public Bike(){}
}
```

In the previous code, the new class is defined. We also define a method called **Bike** that will act as a constructor for the class **Bike**. In other words, every time a new **Bike** is created (or instantiated), this method will be called.

Again, the class is a template that will be used to create objects, and the constructor is the method that is used to create this new object, and to specify, when need be, the default attributes.

While we will see more about the concept of constructors in the next sections, note that constructors do not have a return type and this is what (amongst other aspects) differentiates constructors from other methods.

Object-Oriented Programming & Classes

Next, we will start to modify the class to include the member variables and methods that we introduced and explained earlier on, as follows:

- First, please add two member variables as follows (new code in bold):

```
public class Bike
{
    private float speed;
    private int color;
```

In the previous code, we create two float variables **speed** and **color**. This are member variables that will be used as attributes for any bike created based on the class **Bike**.

- Then add the methods **accelerate** and **turnRight** as follows:

```
public void accelerate()
{
    speed++;
}
public void turnRight()
{
}
```

In the previous code, we create two methods **accelerate** and **turnRight**. They are both of type **void** as they don't return any data.

- Finally add the three other methods **setSpeed**, **getSpeed** and **calculateDistance**.

```
private void calculateDistance()
{
}
public void setSpeed(float newSpeed)
{
    speed = newSpeed;
}
public float getSpeed()
{
    return (speed);
}
```

In the previous code, we add three more methods. Two of them are of type void (**calculateDistance** and **setSpeed**) as they don't return any data. The method **getSpeed** returns the value of the member variable **speed**.

So the full code for the file **Bike.cs** should look as follows:

```
public class Bike
{

    private float speed;
    private int color;
    public Bike(){}

    public void accelerate()
    {
        speed++;
    }
    public void turnRight()
    {
    }
    private void calculateDistance()
    {
    }
    public void setSpeed(float newSpeed)
    {
        speed = newSpeed;
    }
    public float getSpeed()
    {
        return (speed);
    }
}
```

- Once this is done, you can save your code and compile it by pressing the button labelled compile located at the top of the window.

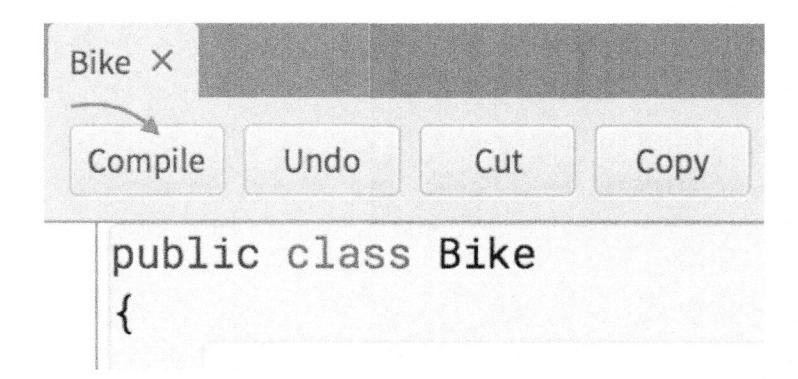

Figure 3-4: Compiling the class Bike

We can now, use the class **Bike** from the **main** method in the file **MyClass** by adding the following lines to the **main** method.

```
Bike myBike = new Bike();
System.out.println("Initial Speed=" + myBike.getSpeed());
myBike.setSpeed(23.0f);
System.out.println("New Speed="+myBike.getSpeed());
```

In the previous code:

- We create new bike
- We then display the initial speed of the new bike.
- The speed of the new bike is increased.
- We display the value of the new speed.

You can now save the file **MyClass**, and compile it.

You should now see, in the Project window that an arrow is now pointing from the class **MyClass** to the class **Bike**, to show that a new **Bike** object is created in the class called **MyClass**.

Object-Oriented Programming & Classes

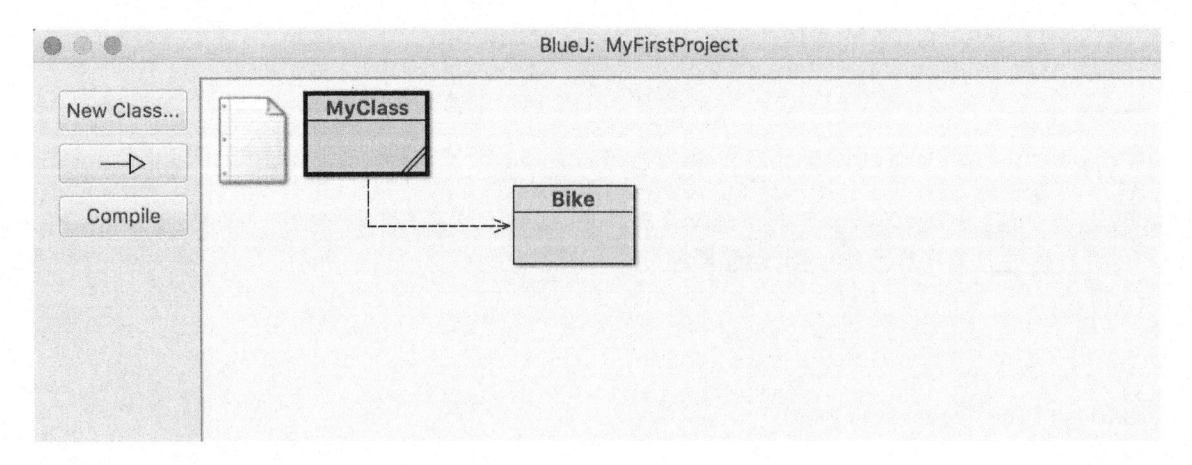

Figure 3-5: Displaying links between classes

So the idea here is to have a main application called **MyClass** that will be using the class called Bike; however, as we have seen earlier, we could also use this class called bike in a different application, hence, saving ourselves some time coding.

- Once this is done, you can run the application as usual by right-clicking on the icon called "**MyClass**" and by selecting the option **void main (String [] parameters)**.

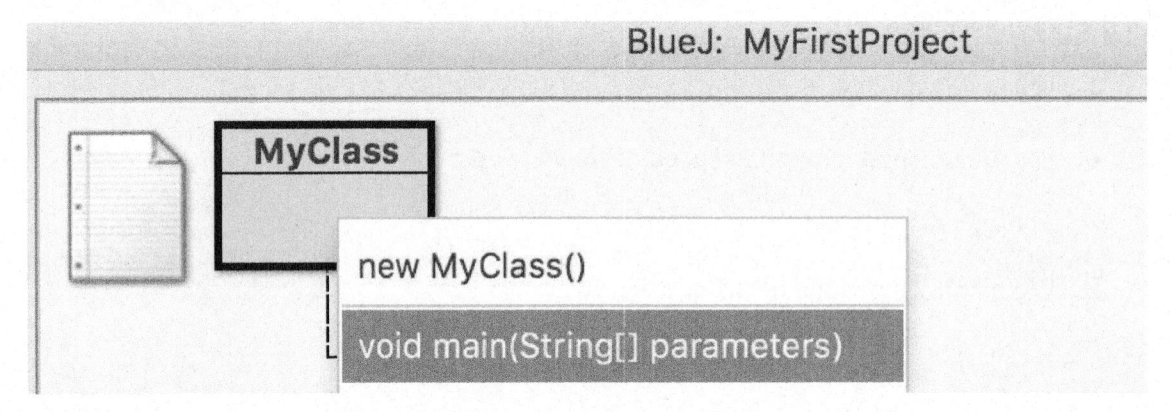

Figure 3-6: Running the application

You should see two messages as in the next figure.

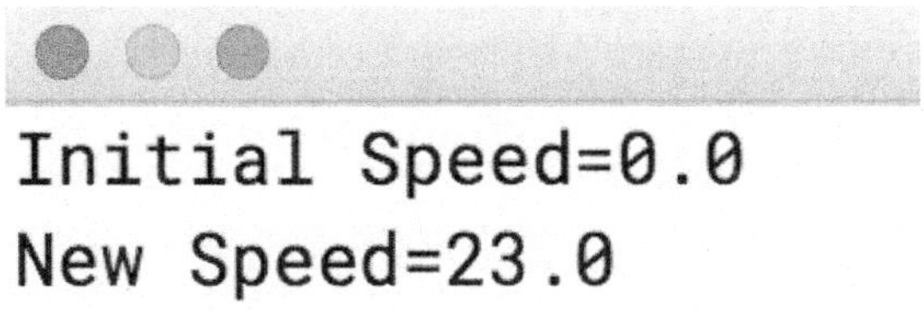

```
Initial Speed=0.0
New Speed=23.0
```

Figure 3-7: Setting the speed

This message makes sense since we created a new bike with a speed of zero initially; we then set its speed to 23.

CONSTRUCTORS

A class usually includes a constructor; a constructor basically is a method that includes a set of instructions that will be used to initialize an object created from this class. As we will see later, classes can have different constructors, each initializing the new object differently. Some may need parameters, and some may not need any parameter at all; but ultimately, all the constructors are used to construct based on the class, in a specific way, usually by setting some of the member variables.

As we have seen in the previous section, when a new object is created, it will, by default, include all the member variables and methods from its class. To create this object, we would use the name of the class, followed by (), as per the next example.

```
Bike myBike = new Bike();
myBike.accelerate();
```

By using the keyword **new**, we implicitly call a constructor from the class Bike. Now, if you have not defined any constructor for your class, this will call the default constructor which will do nothing, except creating a new object from this class.

This being said, you can, if you wish, create one or more constructors for your class. These constructors will, for example, change some of the properties of the new object created at the time it is initialized. For example, a constructor could set these the value for the variables speed and color when it is created.

So, for example, let's say that we would like the color of our bike to be specified when it is created; we could modify the **Bike** class, as follows, by adding the following method:

```
public Bike (int newColor)
{
     color = newColor;
}
```

This is a new constructor as the name of the method is the same as the class. It takes an integer as a parameter; so after modifying the description of our class (as per the code above), we could then create a new **Bike** object as follows:

```
Bike myBike = new Bike(2);
```

We could even specify a second constructor that would include both the color and the speed as follows:

```
public Bike (int newColor, float newSpeed)
{
    color = newColor;
    speed = newSpeed;
}
```

Having multiple constructors can be useful as it allows you to instantiate an object in different ways, depending on the parameter that are already setup, or the ones that you'd like to account for at the initialization stage. In our case, we might just want to create a new bike without specifying its speed or color, or to create a new bike and specify its speed or color at the initialization stage. So having multiple can be convenient in this case.

So, you can have different constructors in your class and the system will determine which constructor that should be called based on the signature of the constructor (i.e., the parameters that should be passed to the method).

For example, let's say that we have two constructors for our **Bike** class, as follows.

```
public Bike (int newColor)
{
    color = newColor;
}


public Bike (int newColor, float newSpeed)
{
    color = newColor;
    speed = newSpeed;
}
```

If a new **Bike** object is created as follows:

```
Bike newBike = new Bike (2)
```

…then the first constructor will be called.

If a new **Bike** object is created as follows:

Object-Oriented Programming & Classes

```
Bike newBike = new Bike (2, 10.0f)
```

...then the second constructor will be called.

You may also wonder what happens if the following code is used if no default constructor has been defined.

```
Bike newBike = new Bike ();
```

In fact, whenever you create your class, a default constructor is also defined (implicitly) and evoked whenever a new object is created using the **new** operator with no arguments. This is called a default constructor. In this case, the default values for each of the types of the numerical member variables are used (e.g., 0 for integers or false for Boolean variables).

> Note that access to constructors is usually public, except in the particular cases where we would like a class not to be instantiated (e.g., for classes that include **static** members only). Also note that, as for member variables, if no access modifiers are specified, these will be **private** by default. This is similar for methods.

Now that this is clear, let's experiment with different constructors.

Please open the file **Bike**.

- Add the following code at the end of the class (before the last closing curly bracket).

```
public int getColor()
{
    return color;


}
public Bike(int newColor)
{
    color = newColor;
}
public Bike(int newColor, float newSpeed)
{
    color = newColor;
    speed = newSpeed;
}
```

In the previous code, we create a method **getColor** that returns the color for the current **Bike**; we also create two additional constructors, each taking different number and types of parameters.

- You can now save and compile your code for the file **Bike**.

Now, we just need to use these constructors.

- In the file **MyClass**, please modify the **main** method as follows (new code in bold):

Object-Oriented Programming & Classes

```
Bike myBike = new Bike();
System.out.println("Initial Speed=" + myBike.getSpeed());
myBike.setSpeed(23.0f);
System.out.println("New Speed="+myBike.getSpeed());
Bike myBike2 = new Bike(2);
System.out.println("The color of Bike2 is " + myBike2.getColor()
+ " and its speed is " + myBike2.getSpeed());
Bike myBike3 = new Bike(10, 3);
System.out.println("The color of Bike3 is " + myBike3.getColor()
+ " and its speed is " + myBike3.getSpeed());
```

In the previous code:

- We create two additional bikes.
- **myBike2** is created using the second constructor, and we pass the number **2** (for its color) to this constructor.
- **myBike3** is created using the third constructor, and we pass the number **10** for its color, as well as the number **3** for its speed.

You can now save your code for the file **MyClass** and run the application, and the following messages should be displayed:

```
Initial Speed=0.0
New Speed=23.0
The color of Bike2 is 2 and its speed is 0.0
The color of Bike3 is 10 and its speed is 3.0
```

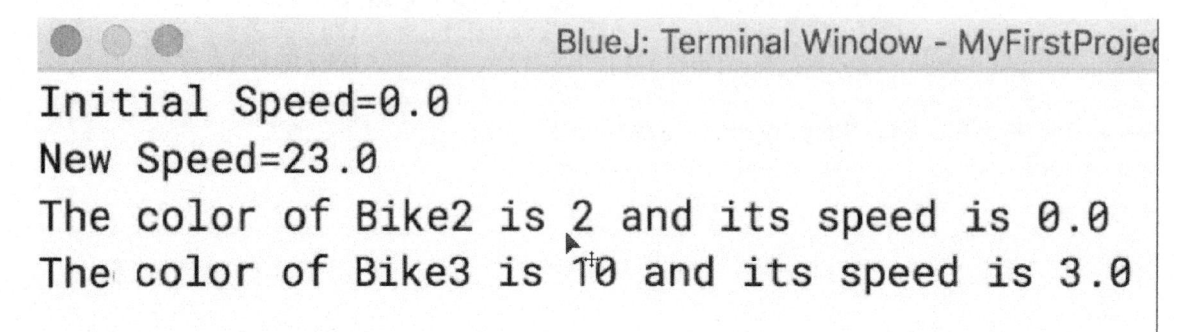

Figure 3-8: Instantiating bikes

So thanks to the previous example, you were able to create two additional constructors for the class Bike. So we have overloaded the default constructor to create other constructors with a different signature, in that they take parameters when called, and each of the two new constructors take a different number and type of parameters. Again this is an object-oriented feature and it makes things easier in that we can create a bike in different ways, using or discarding some of the existing member variables.

STATIC MEMBERS OF A CLASS

The concept of static members provides a great advantage over procedural programming. If you remember the last chapter, we saw how it would be difficult to reuse code between two programmes using a procedural approach, and how OOP made this much easier.

Static methods and variables are a great example of this efficiency; for example, using static methods, you can create a method that can be called from outside the class without the need to instantiate an object, and that can be used to perform some utility tasks. In addition, a static variable is shared between all the instances of the class.

When a variable is declared as static, only one instance of this member exists for a class. So a static variable will be "shared" between instances of this class.

Static variables are often employed to retrieve constants without instantiating a new object. The same applies for static methods: they can be evoked without having to instantiate a new object from a class. This can be very useful if you want to create and avail of tools.

So, let's explore how we could use static functions and variables in our class **Bike**.

We could create a static variable for example, that counts the number of bikes that have been created; a static variable would be ideal in this case, as it would be shared between all instances of the class **Bike**. In other words, whenever a bike is created, it will have access to this variable, and in or case, we would increase its value by one, so that we can keep track of the number of bikes created. Let's see how.

- Please open the file **Bike**.

- Add the following code at the start of the class (new code in bold).

```
public class Bike
{
    private float speed;
    private int color;
    private static int nbBikes;
```

In the previous code, we declare the variable **nbBikes** that will keep track of the number of bikes instantiated (or created) from the class **Bike**. It is private and static, which means that it will be only available from member methods and it will also be shared across instances of the class **Bike**.

Object-Oriented Programming & Classes

- Add the following methods to this class:

```
private void increaseNbBikes()
{
    nbBikes++;
}


public int getNbBikes()
{
    return (nbBikes);
}
```

In the previous code:

- We declare two methods.

- The method **increaseNbBikes** is private, so it will be accessible only from member methods and it will increase the value of the variable **nbBikes** by one every time it is called.

- The method **getNbBikes** is public which means that it will be accessible from outside the class, and return the total number of objects instantiated from the class **Bike**.

We will now modify the three constructors that we have created earlier for the class **Bike**, so that every time a bike is created, the number of bikes is increased accordingly.

- Please modify the first constructor as follows (new code in bold):

```
public Bike()
{
    increaseNbBikes();
}
```

- Please modify the second constructor as follows (new code in bold):

```
public Bike(int newColor)
{
    color = newColor;
    increaseNbBikes();
}
```

- Please modify the third constructor as follows (new code in bold):

```
public Bike(int newColor, float newSpeed)
{
    color = newColor;
    speed = newSpeed;
    increaseNbBikes();
}
```

- Last but not least, modify the **Main** method in the file **MyClass** as follows (new code in bold).

```
public static void Main(String[] args)
{
Bike myBike = new Bike();
System.out.println("Initial Speed=" + myBike.getSpeed());
myBike.setSpeed(23.0f);
System.out.println("New Speed="+myBike.getSpeed());
Bike myBike2 = new Bike(2);
System.out.println("Thecolor of Bike2 is " + myBike2.getColor() +
" and its speed is " + myBike2.getSpeed());
Bike myBike3 = new Bike(10, 3);
System.out.println("Thecolor of Bike3 is " + myBike3.getColor() +
" and its speed is " + myBike3.getSpeed());
System.out.println("Number of Bikes Created: " +
myBike.getNbBikes());
```

You can now save both files (i.e., **MyClass** and **Bike**), compile them, and run the application, and you should see the following message in the console window.

Object-Oriented Programming & Classes

```
                        BlueJ: Terminal Window - MyFirstProject
Initial Speed=0.0
New Speed=23.0
The color of Bike2 is 2 and its speed is 0.0
The color of Bike3 is 10 and its speed is 3.0
Number of Bikes Created: 3
```

Figure 3-9: Using static variables

Finally, we could create a static method for the class **Bike** that could be called without the need to instantiate an object from the class **Bike**, as follows.

- Please add the following method to the class Bike.

```
public static void explainWhatABikeIs()
{
    System.out.println("A bike is a human-powered, pedal-driven, single-track vehicle, having two wheels attached to a frame, one behind the other");
}
```

- Finally, add the following code to the **Main** method in the file **MyClass**.

```
public static void main(String[] parameters)
{
    Bike.explainWhatABikeIs();
```

As you save the files and run the application, you should see a message saying "**A bike is a human-powered, pedal-driven, single-track vehicle, having two wheels attached to a frame, one behind the other**" in the console window.

So here we have managed to create a method that can be used from outside the class bike; so we could, amongst other things, create a new programme that just displays the definition without even instantiating a new bike.

INHERITANCE

I hope everything is clear so far, as we are going to look into a very interesting and important concept for object-oriented programming: inheritance. The main idea behind inheritance is that objects can inherit their properties from other objects (i.e., their parent). As they inherit these properties, they can remain identical to their parent or evolve and overwrite some of these inherited properties. This is very interesting because it makes it possible to minimize the code by creating a class with general properties for all objects sharing similar features, and then, if need be, to overwrite and customize some of these properties for the children.

Let's take the example of vehicles. Vehicles would generally have the following properties:

- Number of wheels.
- Speed.
- Number of passengers.
- Color.
- Capacity to accelerate.
- Capacity to stop.

So we could create the following class for example:

Object-Oriented Programming & Classes

```
class Vehicle
{
    private int nbWheels;
    protected float speed;
    private int nbPassengers;
    private int color;
    public void accelerate()
    {
        speed++;
    }
}
```

These features could apply for example to cars, bikes, motorbikes, or trucks. However, all these vehicles also differ; some of them may or may not have an engine or a steering wheel. So we could create a subclass called **MotorizedVehicle**, based on **Vehicle**, but with specificities linked to the fact that they are motorized. These added attributes could be:

- Engine size.
- Petrol type.
- Petrol levels.
- Ability to fill-up the tank.

The following example illustrates how this class could be created.

```
class MotoredVehicle extends Vehicle
{
    private float engineSize;
    private int petrolType;
    private float petrolLevels;
    public void fillUpTank()
    {
        petrolLevels+=10;
    }
}
```

- When the class is defined, its name is followed by **"extends Vehicle"**. This means that it inherits from the class **Vehicle**. So it will, by default, avail of all the methods and variables already included in the class **Vehicle**.

- We have created a new member method for this class, called **fillUpTank**.

- In the previous example, you may notice that the methods and variables that were defined for the class **Vehicle** do not appear here; this is because they are implicitly added to this new class, since it inherits from the class **Vehicle**.

When using inheritance, the parent is usually referred to as the **base class (or superclass/parent class)** while the child is referred to as the **subclass class**.

Now, while the child inherits "features" from its parents, these can always be modified or, put simply, overwritten.. By default, in Java, all non-static methods are virtual. In other words, as long as a method is declared as not static, it can be overridden by its children. When overriding a method, the keyword **Override** must be used. This is illustrated in the following code.

```
class Vehicle
{
    private int nbWheels;
    protected float speed;
    private int nbPassengers;
    private int color;
    public void accelerate()
    {
        speed++;
    }
}
class MotoredVehicle extends Vehicle
{
    private float engineSize;
    private int petrolType;
    private float petrolLevels;
    private void fillUpTank()
    {
        petrolLevels += 10;
    }
    @Override
    public override void accelerate()
    {
        speed += 10;
    }
}
```

In the previous example, while the method **accelerate** is inherited from the class **Vehicle**, it would normally increase the speed by one. However, by overwriting it in the class **MotoredVehicle**, we make sure that in the case of objects instantiated from the class **MotoredVehicle**, each acceleration increases the speed by 10. We can access the member variable **speed** from the child class **MotoredVehicle** because it has been declared as **protected**.

As we have seen in the previous section, by using inheritance, we can create general purpose classes, for which the behaviour and attributes can be overridden by the children. This, again, has the benefits of saving development time as classes can be reused and or/modified easily.

So let's experiment with inheritance:

- Please create a new class called **Vehicle**: from the main window, press the button labelled **New Class...**

This will create and open a new file called **Vehicle**.

- You can then replace the code automatically generated in the class with the following code.

```
class Vehicle
{
    private int nbWheels;
    protected float speed;
    private int nbPassengers;
    private int color;

    public Vehicle()
    {
    }
    public void accelerate()
    {
        speed++;
    }
    public void displaySpeed()
    {
     System.out.println("Current Speed:"+speed);
    }
}
```

- You can then create a new class called **MotoredVehicle** and replace the code automatically generated with the following code.

```
class MotoredVehicle extends Vehicle
{
    private float engineSize;
    private int petrolType;
    private float petrolLevels;
    public void fillUpTank()
    {
        petrolLevels+=10;
    }
    @Override
    public void accelerate()
    {
      speed+=10;
     }
}
```

In the previous code, you may notice that the method **accelerate** inherited from the class **Vehicle** was overridden so that the speed is increased by 10 after each acceleration (instead of 1).

- Once this is done, you can save and compile both files (i.e., **Vehicle** and **MotoredVehicle**).

- Last but not least, please add this code to the **main** method in the file **MyClass** (you can comment the previous code in this method).

```
public static void main(String[] parameters)
{
    Vehicle v1 = new Vehicle();
    v1.accelerate();
    v1.displaySpeed();
    MotoredVehicle v2 = new MotoredVehicle();
    v2.accelerate();
    v2.displaySpeed();
```

In the previous code:

Object-Oriented Programming & Classes

- We create an instance of the class **Vehicle** and one instance of the class **MotoredVehicle**.

- We call the method **accelerate** for both of these objects (bearing in mind that the **accelerate** method for the **MotoredVehicle** is different to its parent) and display their speed.

Please save your code, compile the file **MyClass** and run the application; you should see the following messages.

```
Current Speed:1.0
Current Speed:10.0
```

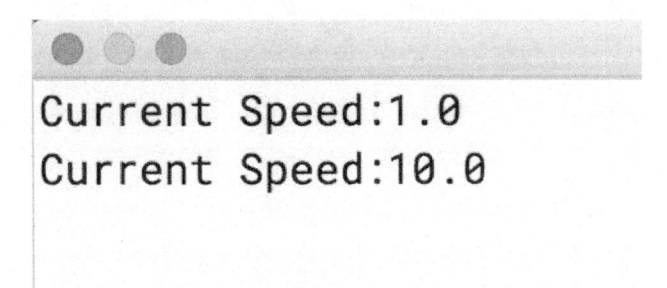

Figure 3-10: Displaying the speed of two different vehicles

So effectively, based on the previous figure we can see that, if you create a motorized vehicle and accelerate this vehicle, its speed is increased by 10, instead of 1 if it was a simple vehicle.

Another interesting thing about inheritance is that it is possible to re-use and adapt the constructor from the base class (the parent). For example, at present the constructor from the class **Vehicle** looks as follows:

```
public Vehicle()
{

}
```

To make it more useful, we could modify it so that it actually initializes some member variables as follows:

[136]

```
public Vehicle()
{
    speed = 0;
    nbWheels = 2;
    nbPassengers = 2;
}
```

So by default, when creating a new **MotoredVehicle** object, it will call this constructor; this being said, when **MotoredVehicle** objects are created, some of their member variables will need to be modified or added; for example, a **MotoredVehicle** object will also need to have an initial value for the variables **engineSize**, **petrolType**, or **petrolLevels**; so to hit two birds with one stone, we could write code that calls the parent constructors to initialize the variables **speed**, **nbWheels**, and **nbPassengers** and that also sets an initial value for the variables **engineSize**, **petrolType**, or **petrolLevels**.

So we could modify the default constructor for the class **MotoredVehicle** as follows:

```
public MotoredVehicle()
{
    super();
    engineSize = 2;
    petrolType = 0;
    petrolLevels = 100;
}
```

In the previous code:

- We define the constructor for the class **MotoredVehicle**.

- We specify that when called, this constructor will, in turn, call the constructor from the base class (i.e., the constructor for the parent class called **Vehicle**) using the keyword **super**.

- If you remember well the constructor from the parent class initializes the speed, the number of wheels along with the number of passengers.

- So by calling the parent constructor using the keyword super, we avoid rewriting the exact same code in the child's constructor.

Object-Oriented Programming & Classes

- After calling the constructor for the base class, the variables **engineSize**, **petrolType** and **petrolLevels** will be initialized.

We could also add a second constructor to the class **MotoredVehicle** as follows:

```
public MotoredVehicle(float newEngineSize, int newPetroltype, int newPetrolLevels)
{
    super();
    engineSize = newEngineSize;
    petrolType = newPetroltype;
    petrolLevels = newPetrolLevels;
}
```

In the previous code:

- We declare a constructor for the class **MotoredVehicle** that takes three parameters.

- We specify that when called, this constructor will, in turn call the constructor from the base class (i.e., the constructor for the parent class called vehicle) using the keyword **super**.

- After this, the variables **engineSize**, **petrolType** and **petrolLevels** will be initialized using the parameters passed to this constructor.

So, as you can see, inheritance can be used to make your code more concise, and save you some time. In the previous example, we saw that by calling the parent constructor, you can avoid to repeat writing code that is already created in the parent class.

There are obviously more concepts linked to inheritance; however, the information provided in this section should get you started easily with this aspect of Java. For more information on inheritance in Java, you can look at the official documentation:

https://docs.oracle.com/Javase/tutorial/Java/concepts/inheritance.html

ACCESSING METHODS AND ACCESS MODIFIERS

The ability to restrict access to (and to hide) variables and methods provides more security to your applications, and is usually referred as **encapsulation**, and this is often achieved through access modifiers.

As we have seen previously, there are different types of access modifiers in Java. These modifiers specify from where a method can be called. These access modifiers can be **public** (no restrictions), **protected** (access limited to the containing class, classes from the same package – a grouping of files -, and subclasses from other packages), **default** (this this the default mode if no access modified is specified; in this case, access is limited to the containing class and classes from the same package) and **private** (access only from the containing class or type).

For example, in the previous example, we have declared the variable **speed** as **protected** so that it can be accessed by the class **Vehicle** and its children, including the class **MotoredVehicle**.

POLYMORPHISM (GENERAL CONCEPTS)

The word polymorphism takes its meaning from **poly** (several) and **morph** (shape); so it literally means several forms. In Object-Oriented Programming, it refers to the ability to process objects differently (or more specifically) depending on their data type or class.

In Java, polymorphism can make it possible to create methods with the same name but with a different signature (i.e., different number and types of parameters) and this is usually called **overloading**.

Polymorphism in Java also makes it possible for children classes to modify a method inherited from their parents and this is usually called **overriding**, as we have seen earlier in this chapter.

Let's take the example of performing an addition. If we want to add two numbers, we make an algebraic addition (e.g., 1 + 2). However, adding two **String** variables may mean concatenating them (adding them one after the other).

For example, adding the text "**Hello**" and the text "**World**" would result in the text "**HelloWorld**". As you can see, the way an operation is performed on different data types may vary and produce different results. So again, with polymorphism, we will be able to customize methods (or operations) so that data is processed based on the parameters passed to this method o. So, let's look at the following code which illustrates how this can be done in Java.

For example, we could create two methods called **decelerate** for the class **Vehicle**, but each could take different number and types of parameters, as follows:

```
public void decelerate()
{
    speed--;
}
public void decelerate(float decrease)
{
    speed-=decrease;
}
```

In the previous code, we create two member methods with the same name but each with different parameters:

- The first method called **decelerate** takes no parameter and decreases the speed by one when called.

- The second method has the same name; it takes one parameter that is used to decrease the speed by the amount specified in the parameter.

- While these two methods have the same name, they can be differentiated thanks to their parameters' list (i.e., the number and the types of the parameters).

- If the method decelerate is called for any instance of the associated object, the system will know which one to use based on the type of number of parameters were passed to the method.

To experiment with this concept, you could do the following:

- Add these methods to the class **Vehicle**.

```
public void decelerate()
{
    speed--;
}
public void decelerate(float decrease)
{
    speed-=decrease;
}
```

- Save and compile the file **Vehicle**.

Object-Oriented Programming & Classes

- Add the following code to the **main** method in the file **MyClass** (new code in bold).

```
MotoredVehicle v2 = new MotoredVehicle();
v2.accelerate();
v2.displaySpeed();

v2.decelerate();
v2.decelerate();
v2.displaySpeed();

v2.decelerate(8);
v2.displaySpeed();
```

In the previous code:

- Before the new code the speed of **v2** should be **10** as it has been accelerated trough the method **accelerate** available from the **MotoredVehicle** class.

- We access one of the decelerate method twice; since we don't pass any parameter, the first method (the one without any parameter) will be called, and the speed will be decreased by 1 twice. So the new speed should be **8**.

- We then access one of the decelerate method once; since we pass a parameter (i.e., **8**), the **second** method (the one with a parameter) will be called, and the speed will be decreased by **8**. So the new speed should be **0**.

You can save your code, compile it, and run the application; you should then see the following messages:

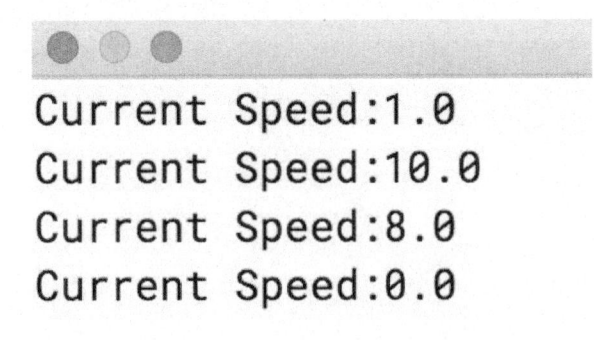

```
Current Speed:1.0
Current Speed:10.0
Current Speed:8.0
Current Speed:0.0
```

Figure 3-11: Using polymorphism

[142]

PACKAGES AND NAMESPACES

In Java, it is possible to group several files and classes under a specific directory (or package) to avoid ambiguity and to clarify where a specific class that we want to use originates from.

By default, Java includes several built-in packages with classes that can be used for a specific purpose; for example, the package **Java.io** can be used to deal with inputs and outputs, and the package **Java.util.zip** can be used to deal with zip files.

When a package has been created, the classes within can be imported and used accordingly using the **import** directive.

For example, in the first part of this book, we used the class called **Scanner** to capture the input from the user. The class called **Scanner** is part of the package called **Java.util**; so, to be able to use it, we have added the following code at the start of the class **MyClass**.

```
import Java.util.Scanner;
```

This way, when we use the **Scanner** class, as illustrated in the next code, Java knows that we refer to the class **Scanner** that is located in the package **Java.util**.

```
Scanner sc= new Scanner (System.in);
```

Similarly, the class called **Arrays** is part of the package called **Java.util**; so, to be able to use it, we have added the following code at the start of the class **MyClass**.

```
import Java.util.Arrays;
```

This way, when we use the **Arrays** class, as illustrated in the next code, Java knows that we refer to the class **Arrays** that is located in the package **Java.util**.

```
Arrays.sort(test);
```

Another very useful thing is to be able to import several classes from the same package at once. For example, if we were to import several classes from the package **Java.util**, we could also import all of the classes within this package by using the following syntax:

```
import Java.util.*;
```

LISTS

As we have seen in the previous sections, it is sometimes useful to employ arrays. However, when you are dealing with a large amount of data, or data that is meant to grow overtime, lists may be more useful, as they include built-in tools to sort and organize your data. So, you don't always need to use lists; however, they may be more efficient to organize your data, especially for large and evolving data sets.

So let's look into **Lists**.

- You can declare a list as follows:

```
ArrayList <int> myList;
```

- The declaration follows the syntax:

```
ArrayList <type> nameOfVariable;
```

So you could create a list of **integers**, **Strings**, or **Vehicle** objects.

Once the list has been created, Java offers several built-in methods that make it possible to manipulate a list, including:

- **add**: adds an item at the end of the list.
- **clear**: removes all elements from the list.
- **remove**: removes an item from the list.
- **size**: returns the number of items in a list.

Each element in the list has a default index that is relative to when it was first added to the list; the earlier the item is added to the list and the lower the index. So the first item added to the list will have, by default, the index 0, the second item will have the index 1, and so on.

Let's look at an example:

```
ArrayList <String> listOfNames = new ArrayList<String> ();
listOfNames.add ("Mary");
listOfNames.add ("Paul");
System.out.println("Size of List " + listOfNames.size());
//this will display "Size of list 2"
listOfNames.remove("Paul");
System.out.println("Size of List after removing " +
listOfNames.size());
```

In the previous code:

- We create a new list of **String** variables.
- We then add two elements to the list, the Strings **Mary** and **Paul**.
- We display the size of the list before and after an item has been removed from the list.

We could now experiment with the creation of a list.

- Please add the following code (if you haven't already done so) to the beginning of the file **MyClass**.

```
import java.util.Arrays;
```

- Please add the following code to the **main** method in the file **MyClass**.

```
ArrayList <String> listOfNames = new ArrayList<String> ();
listOfNames.add ("Mary");
listOfNames.add ("Paul");
listOfNames.add("John");
listOfNames.add("Zoe");
listOfNames.add("Hannah");
System.out.println("Size of List: " + listOfNames.size());
listOfNames.remove("Paul");
System.out.println("Size of List after removing Paul: " +
listOfNames.size());
```

In the previous code:

Object-Oriented Programming & Classes

- We declare a list of Strings and add five names to it.
- We then remove the first element of the list (i.e., **Paul**).
- We also display the size of the list before removing **Paul** and after.

You can now save your code, and run the application; you should see the following messages.

```
Size of List: 5
Size of List after removing Paul: 4
```

Next, we could try to sort this list alphabetically; to do so, we will use the method called **sort**.

- Please add the following code to the **main** method in the file called **MyClass**.

```
System.out.println("List before sort");
for (int i = 0; i < listOfNames.size(); i++)
{

    System.out.println(listOfNames.get(i));
}
Collections.sort(listOfNames);
System.out.println("List after sort");
for (int i = 0; i < listOfNames.size(); i++)
{

    System.out.println(listOfNames.get(i));
}
```

In the previous code:

- We create a loop that will go from **0** to the size of the **list -1**.
- While in this loop, we display the name of the current element at the index **i**.
- Effectively, we loop through the list and display the name of each element within.
- Following this, we sort the list using the method **sort** from the class **Collections**. This class can be used to sort **ArrayList** objects.

- Once this is done, we display the element of the list that has just been sorted using the method **get**.

You can now save your code, and run the application; you should see the following messages in the console window.

```
List before sort
Mary
John
Zoe
Hannah
List after sort
Hannah
John
Mary
Zoe
```

As you can see, the list has been sorted in alphabetical order, with **Hannah** becoming the first element and **Zoe** becoming the last one.

There are many more methods available for lists, and you can see (and experiment with) them on the official page:

https://docs.oracle.com/Javase/8/docs/api/Java/util/ArrayList.html

HASHMAPS

Lists are very useful, and **HashMap**, which are a special type of list, take this concept a step further. With **HashMaps**, you can define a dataset with different records, and each record is accessible through a key instead of an index; for example, let's consider a class of students, each with a first name, a last name, and a student number. To represent and manage this data, we could create code similar to the following:

```
public class Student
{
    public String firstName;
    public String lastName;
    public Student(String fName, String lName)
    {
        firstName = fName;
        lastName = lName;
    }
}
```

- We could then create code that uses this class to store the details of several students as follows:

```
HashMap<String, Student> students = new HashMap<String, Student>();
students.put("ST123",new Student("Mary", "Black"));
students.put("ST124",new Student("John", "Hennessy"));
System.out.println("Name of student ST124 is " + students.get("ST124").firstName);
```

In the previous code:

- We declare a HashMap of **Students**.
- When declaring the HashMap: the first parameter, which is a **String**, is used as an **index** or a **key**; this index will be the **student id**.
- The second parameter will be an object of type **Student**.

- So effectively we create a link between the **key** and the **Student** object.

- We then add students to our HashMap.

- When using the **add** method, the first parameter is the **key** (or the **student id** in our case: **ST123** or **ST124** here), and the second parameter is the student object. This student object is created by calling the constructor of the class **Student** and by passing relevant parameters to the constructor, such as the student's first name and last name.

- Finally, we print the **first name** of a specific student based on its **student id**.

As for lists, HashMaps have several built-in methods that make it easier to manipulate them, including:

- **add**: to add a new item to the HashMap.

- **containsKey**: to check if a record with a specific key exists in the HashMap.

- **remove**: to remove an item from the HashMap.

Let's experiment with the creation of HashMaps.

- Please create a new class called **Student**: from the main window select **Edit | New Class**, then choose the option **Class** and type **Student** in the field called **Class Name**.

- This will create a new file called **Student**.

- Replace the existing code with the following (new code in bold).

```
public class Student
{
    public String firstName;
    public String lastName;
    public Student(String fName, String lName)
    {
        firstName = fName;
        lastName = lName;
    }
}
```

- Once this is done, we can modify the **main** method in the file **MyClass** by adding the following code:

```
HashMap<String, Student> students = new HashMap<String, Student>();
students.put("ST123",new Student("Mary", "Black"));
students.put("ST124",new Student("John", "Hennessy"));
System.out.println("Name of student ST124 is " + students.get("ST124").firstName);
```

- Once this is done, we can save both files, compile them, and run the application; you should see the following message in the console window:

```
Name of student ST124 is John
```

LEVEL ROUNDUP

In this chapter, we have learned some interesting concepts related to Java and Object-Oriented Programming. We also learnt how to define and to use classes, along with member variables and methods. Along the way, we also looked at other programming concepts such as variables, loops, and conditional statements. So, we have covered considerable ground to get you started with Java!

Checklist

> You can consider moving to the next stage if you can do the following:
>
> - Understand the concept of Object-Oriented Programming.
>
> - Understand the meaning of classes, member variables and member methods.
>
> - Understand the role of a constructor.
>
> - Understand the role of access modifiers.

Quiz

Now, let's check your knowledge! Please answer the following questions or specify if these statements are either correct or incorrect (the solutions are on the next page).

1. A method of type void doesn't return any data.
2. A public variable is accessible from anywhere in the application.
3. A private method is only accessible from within the same class.
4. A protected method is accessible by the children of class.
5. Several constructors can be created for a given class.
6. Methods with the same name can be defined for a given class.
7. By default, children of a class inherit from their parents' member methods and variables.
8. A static member method can be called without the need to instantiate an object from a given class.
9. A child class can override one of its parents' method.
10. Using a list, rather than arrays, can be more appropriate when dealing with data that grows and evolves dynamically.

Solutions to the Quiz

1. TRUE.
2. TRUE.
3. TRUE.
4. TRUE.
5. TRUE.
6. TRUE.
7. TRUE.
8. TRUE.
9. TRUE.
10. TRUE.

4
CREATING A WORD GUESSING GAME

"Most good programmers do programming not because they expect to get paid or get adulation by the public, but because it is fun to program."

- Linus Torvalds

In this section, we will use our skills to create a word-guessing game with the following features:

- A word will be picked at random from an existing list.
- The letters of the word will be hidden.
- The players will try to guess each letter by pressing a letter on their keyboard.
- Once a letter has been discovered, it will then be displayed onscreen.
- The player has a limited number of attempts to guess the word.

So, after completing this chapter, you will be able to:

- Pick a random word.
- Process and assess the letters pressed by the player.
- Display the letters that were correctly guessed by the player.
- Track and display the score.
- Check when the player has used too many guesses.

DETECTING AND PROCESSING THE USER INPUT

In this section, we will implement the main features of the game, that is:

- Create a new word to be guessed.
- Count the number of letters in this word.
- Display corresponding empty text fields.
- Wait for the user to press a key (i.e., a letter) on the keyboard.
- Detect the key pressed by the user.
- Display the corresponding letters in the word to be guessed onscreen.

So let's start.

- Please create a new class called **MyGame**.
- Add the following code at the start of the class (new code in bold).

```
static private String wordToGuess = "";
static private int lengthOfWordToGuess;
static private char [] lettersToGuess;
static private boolean [] lettersGuessed;
static private char [] lettersDiscoveredSoFar;

public static void main (String [] arguments)
{

}
```

In the previous code:

- We declare four new variables.
- **wordToGuess** will be used to store the word to be guessed.
- **lengthOfWordToBeGuessed** will store the number of letters in this word.

Creating a Word Guessing Game

- **lettersToGuess** is an array of characters including every single letter from the word to be discovered by the player.

- **letterGuessed** is an array of Boolean variables used to determine which of the letters in the word to guess were actually guessed correctly by the player.

- **lettersDiscoveredSoFar** is an array of characters that will be used to display the letters that the player has managed to guess.

- We also create the method main that will be the entry point for our game.

Next, we will create a method that will be used to initialize the game.

- Please add the following function to the class.

```java
static void initGame()
{
    wordToGuess = "Elephant";
    lettersDiscoveredSoFar = wordToGuess.toCharArray();
    lengthOfWordToGuess = wordToGuess.length();
    wordToGuess = wordToGuess.toUpperCase ();
    lettersGuessed = new boolean [lengthOfWordToGuess];
    lettersToGuess = new char[lengthOfWordToGuess];
    lettersToGuess = wordToGuess.toCharArray ();
    for (int i = 0; i < lettersDiscoveredSoFar.length; i++)
    {
        lettersDiscoveredSoFar[i] = '_';
    }

    System.out.println(""+new String (lettersDiscoveredSoFar));
}
```

In the previous code:

- We declare a function called **initGame**; this function is static so that it can be called from the static function **main**.

- In this function, we initialize the variable **wordToGuess**; this will be the word **Elephant** for the time being.

- We then capitalize all the letters in this word; as we will see later in this chapter, this will make it easier to match the letter typed by the user with the letters in the word to guess.

- We then initialize the array called **lettersToGuess** and **lettersGuessed**.

> Note that for Boolean variables, the default value, if they have not been initialized, is **false**. As a result, all variables in the array called **lettersGuessed** will initially be set to false by default.

- We initialize the array **lettersDiscoverdSoFar** so that the word to guess is displayed as "_ _ _ _ _ _ _ _" initially.

- Finally, we convert the array **lettersDiscovereSoFar** to a String and display its content as "_ _ _ _ _ _ _ _".

Once this function has been created, we will need to process the user's input; for this purpose, we will create a function that will do the following:

- Detect the letter that was pressed by the player on the keyboard.

- Check if this letter is part of the word to guess.

- In this case, check if this letter has **not** already been guessed by the player.

- In this case, display the corresponding letter onscreen.

Let's write the corresponding code.

- Please add this line of code at the very start of the class.

```
import Java.util.Scanner;
```

This is to import the class **Scanner** that we will use to read the user's input.

- Please add the following function to the class **MyGame**:

Creating a Word Guessing Game

```
static void checkKeyboard()
{
    Scanner sc = new Scanner(System.in);
    System.out.println("Please enter a new letter:");
    char newLetter =  sc.next().charAt(0);
    newLetter = Character.toUpperCase(newLetter);
      if (Character.isLetter('a'))
      {
          for (int i=0; i < lengthOfWordToGuess; i++)
          {
              if (!lettersGuessed [i])
              {
                  if (lettersToGuess [i] == 'A')
                  {
                      lettersGuessed [i] = true;

                      lettersDiscoveredSoFar[i] = 'A';
                  }
              }
          }
      }
    System.out.println(""+new String (lettersDiscoveredSoFar));
}
```

In the previous code:

- We declare the function called **checkKeyBoard**.

- We ask the user to enter a letter.

- Regardless of the String entered by the user, we will only store the first letter entered.

[158]

```
sc.next().charAt(0)
```

- We then store this letter in the variable called **newLetter** and convert it to upper case, so that it can be checked against the letters of the word to be guessed, which are already stored in upper case.

- We then create a loop that goes through all the letters of the word to be guessed; this is done from the first letter (i.e., at the index 0) to the last one.

- We check if this letter has already been guessed.

- If it is **not** the case, we check whether this letter is **A**.

- If this is the case, we then indicate that this letter (i.e., the letter **A**) was found.

- We then display the corresponding letter onscreen.

Last but not least, we just need to be able to call this function to initialize the game and to also process the user's inputs.

- Please add the following code to the **main** function (new code in bold).

```
public static void main (String [] arguments)
{
    initGame();
    checkKeyboard();
}
```

So at this stage, we have all the necessary functions to start our game; so you can save and compile the class **MyGame** and execute it. As the programme is running, you will be asked to enter a letter and if you press the **A** key on the keyboard, the letter **A** should also be displayed onscreen, as it is part of the word **Elephant**.

```
● ● ●
--------
Please enter a new letter:
a
_____A__
```

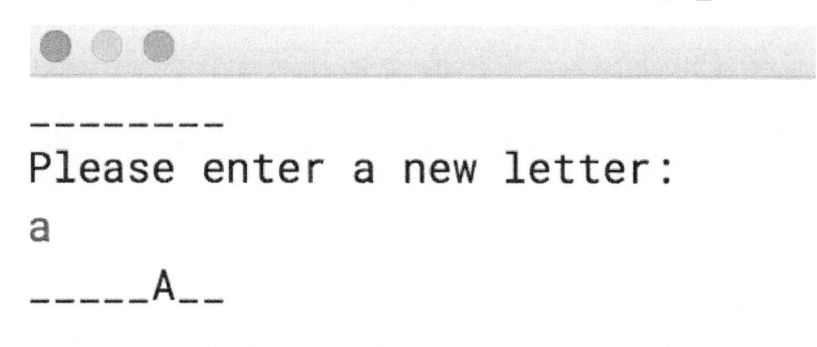

Figure 4-1: Detecting the key pressed

Creating a Word Guessing Game

So, this is working properly, and we could easily add more code to detect the other keys; we could also try to ensure that the key pressed is a letter. So we will create a new method that will involve the following:

- Check if a key was pressed.
- Check if this key is a letter.
- Proceed as previously to check whether this letter is part of the word to be guessed.
- Stop the game after a maximum number of attempts has been reached.

So let's get started:

- Please add the following code at the beginning of the class **MyGame**.

```
static private int nbAttempts = 0;
static private final int maxNbAttemps = 5;
```

- Please create a new function called **checkKeyBoard2**, as follows:

```java
static void checkKeyboard2()
{
    String guessingString;
    Scanner sc = new Scanner(System.in);
    System.out.println("Please enter a new letter:");
    char newLetter =  sc.next().charAt(0);
    nbAttempts++;

    newLetter = Character.toUpperCase(newLetter);
    int asciiCode = (int) newLetter;

      if (asciiCode>=65 && asciiCode <=90)
      {
            for (int i=0; i < lengthOfWordToGuess; i++)
            {
                  if (!lettersGuessed [i])
                  {
                        if (lettersToGuess [i] == newLetter)
                        {
                              lettersGuessed [i] = true;

                              lettersDiscoveredSoFar[i] = newLetter;
                        }
                  }
            }
      }
      System.out.println(""+new String (lettersDiscoveredSoFar));
      if (nbAttempts <= maxNbAttemps)checkKeyboard2();
}
```

In the previous code:

Creating a Word Guessing Game

- We increase the value of the variable **nbAttempts** every time the user enters a letter.

- We then check that this character is actually a letter. This is done using the integer value associated with the letter entered; this corresponds to an integer value between **65** and **90**.

- Once this is done, we check if we have reached the maximum number of attempts.

The last thing we need to do is to call the function **chekKeyboard2** instead of the function **checkKeyboard** by amending the **main** function as follows (new code in bold):

```
public static void main (String [] arguments)
{
    initGame();
    checkKeyboard2();
}
```

That's it!

Once this is done, please save your code, check that it is error-free and test the **Scene**. As you press the keys **E**, **L**, **P** and **A**, you should see that they now appear onscreen.

```
BlueJ: Terminal Window - MyFirstProject
--------
Please enter a new letter:
e
E_E_____
Please enter a new letter:
l
ELE_____
Please enter a new letter:
p
ELEP____
Please enter a new letter:
h
ELEPH___
Please enter a new letter:
```

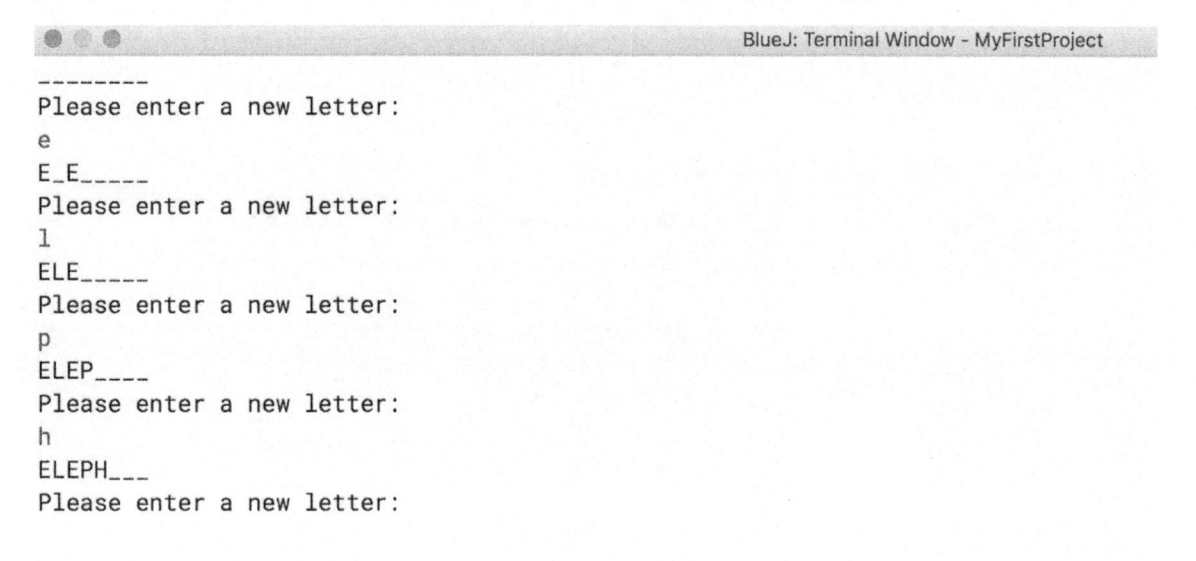

Figure 4-2: Detecting all the keys pressed

CHOOSING RANDOM WORDS

At this stage, the game works properly and the letters that the player has guessed are displayed onscreen; this being said, it would be great to add more challenge by selecting the word to guess at random from a list of pre-defined words. So in the next section, we will learn to do just that; we will start by choosing a word from an array.

So let's get started.

- Please open the class **MyGame.**
- Add the following code at the beginning of the class.

```
static private String [] wordsToGuess = new String [] {"car",
"elephant","autocar" };
```

In the previous code, we declare an array of String variables and we add three words to it.

- Please add the following code at the beginning of the class:

```
import Java.util.Random;
```

In the previous code, we import the class **Random** that can also be used to generate random numbers. Using this class, and amongst other advantages provided by this class, it makes it easier to generate random integers compared to the method **Math.random**.

This is because the number generated in this case (i.e., using the class **Random**) is already an integer, whereas when you use the method **Math.random**, the number generated needs to be multiplied to be able to obtain a random integer.

- Please add the following code to the function **initGame** (new code in bold).

```
//wordToGuess = "Elephant";
Random rand = new Random();
int randomNumber = rand.nextInt(wordsToGuess.length);
wordToGuess = wordsToGuess [randomNumber];
```

In the previous code:

- We comment the previous code.
- We create an object from the class **Random**.

- We create a random number that will range from **0** to the length of the array using the class **Random**. So in our case, because we have three elements in this array, this random number will range from **0** to **2**.

- We then set the variable called **wordToGuess** to one of the words included in the array called **wordsToGuess**; this word will be picked at random based on the variable called **randomNumber**.

You can now save, compile and execute your code, and you should see that a word has been chosen from the array.

TRACKING THE SCORE AND THE NUMBER OF ATTEMPTS

So at this stage, we have a game were we generate random words that need to be guessed by the player. So we will start to finalize our game by adding the following features:

- Display the number of guesses.
- Set and display the maximum number of attempts.
- Detect if all the letters in the word to be guessed were found.
- Restart the game with a new word whenever the previous word has been guessed.
- Display a message when the user has failed to guess the word.

First, we will update the score.

- Please open the file called **MyGame**.
- Add this code at the beginning of the class.

```
private static int score = 0;
```

- Modify the function **checkKeyboard2** as follows (new code in bold):

```
if (lettersToGuess [i] == newLetter)
{
    lettersGuessed [i] = true;
    score++;
    lettersDiscoveredSoFar[i] = newLetter;
}
```

In the previous code, we just increase the score by one every time the player has guessed a letter correctly.

- Please add the following code at the end of the method **checkKeyboard2** (new code in bold).

Creating a Word Guessing Game

```
System.out.println("Your score is now "+score);
System.out.println(""+new String (lettersDiscoveredSoFar));
if (nbAttempts <= maxNbAttemps)checkKeyboard2();
```

In the previous code, we display the current score.

Please save your code, and compile it. As you execute it, you should see that the score is displayed

```
_ _ _
Please enter a new letter:
c
Your score is now 1
C _ _
Please enter a new letter:
```

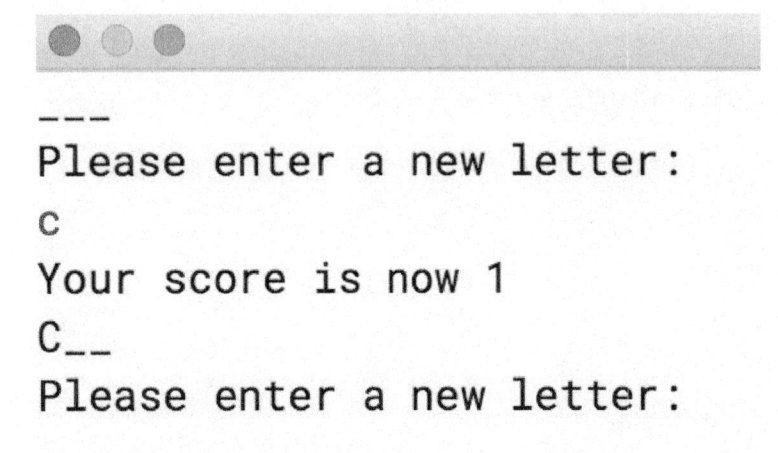

Figure 4-3: Displaying the score

Now, the last thing we need to do is to check whether the player has guessed the word using less than the maximum number of attempts allowed; if this is the case, a **congratulation message** will be displayed; otherwise, if the player has failed to guess the word within the maximum number of attempts allowed, another message will be displayed instead.

- Please add the following code to the function **checkKeyboard2** (new code in bold).

```
System.out.println("Your score is now "+score);
System.out.println(""+new String (lettersDiscoveredSoFar));
if (nbAttempts <= maxNbAttemps)checkKeyboard2();
else
{
    System.out.println("Sorry, you just lost!; would you like to start agin (y/n)?");
    sc = new Scanner(System.in);
    char answer= sc.next().charAt(0);
    if (answer == 'y') main (new String [3]);
}
```

In the previous code:

- We check whether we have reached the maximum number of attempts.

- If we have not reached this number, then the user is asked to enter another letter by calling the method **checkKeyboard2**.

- If we have reached the maximum number of attempts, then we display a message to the user indicating that s/he has lost, and offering him/her to restart.

You can save and compile this code; as you execute the code and enter several erroneous entries (i.e., letter that do not belong to the word to be guessed), the system will let you know that you have lost and offer you to restart a new game.

Creating a Word Guessing Game

```
BlueJ: Terminal Window - MyFirstProject
Your score is now 2
__T___R
Please enter a new letter:
t
Your score is now 2
__T___R
Please enter a new letter:
t
Your score is now 2
__T___R
Please enter a new letter:
t
Your score is now 2
__T___R
Please enter a new letter:
t
Your score is now 2
__T___R
Sorry, you just lost!; would you like to start agin (y/n)?
```

Figure 4-4: Restarting the game when the user has lost

Next, we will create code that will assess whether the player has managed to guess all the letters in the word. For this purpose, we will do the following:

- Create a function that will be called whenever the player has correctly guessed a letter.

- This function will check if all the letters were guessed accurately.

- In this case, it will save the word to be guessed, and then display it onscreen.

So let's create this function:

- Please open the file **MyGame**.

- Add the following method at the end of the class.

```
static void checkIfWordwasFound()
{
    Boolean condition = true;
    for (int i = 0; i < lengthOfWordToGuess; i++)
    {
        condition = condition && lettersGuessed [i];
    }
    if (condition)
    {
        System.out.println("Well Done!; would you like to start agin (y/n)?");
        Scanner sc = new Scanner(System.in);
        char answer= sc.next().charAt(0);
        if (answer == 'y') main (new String [3]);
    }
}
```

In the previous code:

- We define a function called **checkIfWordWasFound**.

- We then declare a Boolean variable called **condition** that will be used to determine if all the letters were found.

- This variable called **condition** is initially set to true.

- We then go through each variable of the array called **letterGuessed** to check the letters that were guessed correctly by the player. If one of the word's letters was not found (i.e., even just one), the variable called **condition** will be set to false.

- The following code effectively performs a logical **AND** between all the variables of the array **lettersGuessed**, as all of them need to be true (i.e., found) for the variable **condition** to be **true**; so this is the same as saying "**if letter1 was guessed, and letter2 was guessed and letter3 was guessed, ..., and the last letter was guessed then the condition is true**"

```
condition = condition && lettersGuessed [i];
```

- If the variable **condition** is **true**, we then ask the player whether s/he wants to restart the game.

Creating a Word Guessing Game

- We then display a congratulation message and ask the user whether s/he want to restart the game.

We can now add a call to this function from the **checkKeyboard2** function, as follows (new code in bold):

```
if (lettersToGuess [i] == newLetter)
{
    lettersGuessed [i] = true;
    score++;
    checkIfWordWasFound ();
```

You can now compile your code and execute it; after guessing all the letters from the mysterious word, a congratulation message should be displayed and you will be asked whether you'd like to restart the game.

```
                                        BlueJ: Terminal Window - MyFirstProject
AU___A_
Please enter a new letter:
t
Your score is now 4
AUT__A_
Please enter a new letter:
o
Your score is now 5
AUTO_A_
Please enter a new letter:
c
Your score is now 6
AUTOCA_
Please enter a new letter:
r
Well Done!; would you like to start agin (y/n)?
y
--------
Please enter a new letter:
```

Figure 4-5: Congratulating the player

LEVEL ROUNDUP

In this chapter, we have learned to create a simple word guessing game where the player can guess the letters of a random word. Along the way, we have learned a few interesting skills including: generating random numbers, or detecting the player's input. So, we have covered considerable ground to get you started with your first word game!

Checklist

You can consider moving to the next stage if you can do the following:

- Create random numbers.
- Create an array of String or Boolean variables.
- Detect the keys pressed by the player.

Creating a Word Guessing Game

Quiz

Now, let's check your knowledge! Please answer the following questions (the answers are included in the resource pack) or specify if these statements are either correct or incorrect.

1. The following code will declare an array of integers.

```
int [] i = new int [];
```

2. The following code will declare and initialize an array of String variables:

```
String [] wordsToGuess = new String [] {"car",
"elephant","autocar"};
```

3. The class **Scanner** can be used to read the keys entered by the user.

4. The following code will display the number of characters in the String **Hello**.

```
String s = "Hello";
print(s.length);
```

5. A **char** variable can be used to store a name with more than two letters.

6. A **String** variable can be used to store a name with more than two letters.

7. It is possible to generate a random number in Java using the method **Math.random**.

8. The first element of an array starts at the index 1.

9. The first element of an array starts at the index 0.

10. It is possible to generate a random number in Java using the class **Random.**

Answers to the Quiz

1. TRUE.
2. TRUE.
3. TRUE.
4. FALSE. It should read **String**.

```
String s = "Hello";
```

5. FALSE (only one character is stored).
6. TRUE.
7. TRUE.
8. FALSE.
9. TRUE.
10. TRUE.

Challenge 1

Now that you have managed to complete this chapter and that you have created your game, you could improve it by doing the following:

- Set the number of attempts to the number of letters in the word to be guessed.
- Add more words to be guessed in the array.

Challenge 2

Another interesting challenge could be as follows:

- Create a two dimensional array of words to be guessed. The first array could deal with the names of animals, and the second array could deal with the names of cities.
- Ensure that words to be guessed are picked randomly from the first or the second array.

5
THANK YOU

I would like to thank you for completing this book. I trust that you feel more confident with Java now. This book is the first in the series "**Java from Zero to Proficiency**", so it may be time to move on to the next books where you will get started with even more Java.

So that the book can be constantly improved, I would really appreciate your feedback. So, ***please leave me a helpful review on Amazon*** letting me know what you thought of the book and also send me an email (learntocodewithpat@gmail.com) with any suggestions you may have. I read and reply to every email. Thanks so much!

Printed in Great Britain
by Amazon